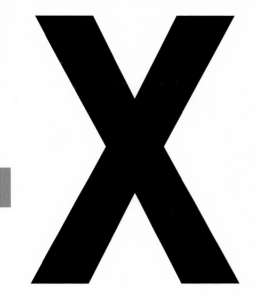

X

JENNY McCARTHY'S OPEN BOOK

Jenny McCarthy

with Neal Karlen

ReganBooks
An Imprint of HarperPerennial
A Division of HarperCollinsPublishers

Photography and art credits appear on page 232.

"If I Were President" questionnaire on page 23 reprinted from *George* magazine, July 1997.

JEN-X: JENNY MCCARTHY'S OPEN BOOK. Copyright © 1997 by Jenny McCarthy. All rights reserved. Printed in the United States of America. No part of this book may be used or reproduced in any manner whatsoever without written permission except in the case of brief quotations embodied in critical articles and reviews. For information address HarperCollins Publishers, Inc., 10 East 53rd Street, New York, NY 10022.

HarperCollins books may be purchased for educational, business, or sales promotional use. For information please write: Special Markets Department, HarperCollins Publishers, Inc., 10 East 53rd Street, New York, NY 10022.

FIRST EDITION

Designed by Ph.D

ISBN 0-06-039233-9

97 98 99 00 01 ❖/RRD-C 10 9 8 7 6 5 4 3 2 1

Dedication

For Ray Manzella, my manager and soul mate who guided me through the perils of Hollywood like a true star-maker, and my family, who has always stood by my side

Acknowledgments

Thanks to Judith Regan, Neal Karlen, everyone at Ph.D, Robyn Forest, Julie Lewis, Linda McCarthy, Joanne McCarthy, Amy McCarthy, Lynette McCarthy, Dan McCarthy, Leigh Brecheen, Tom Collier, Dave Feldman, Susan Bender, William Hawkes, Peggy Sirota, Moshe Brakha, Paul Olsewski, Joe Russo, and Judy McGrath.

The purpose of a relationship is to decide what part of yourself you would like to see "show up," not what part of another you can capture and hold.
—**Neale Donald Walsch,** *Conversations with God*

contents

rags

↓

farts

↓

riches

Okay, let's get one thing straight right from the start, before we begin getting into the meat and potatoes of my inspiring story of rags to farts to riches and farts. Yes, my real name is Jenny McCarthy. Three years ago I was an over-weight, big-haired, lower-middle-class total loser from the South Side of Chicago who'd dropped out of Southern Illinois University because I was $20,000 in debt on credit cards and couldn't afford to pay either my rent or my tuition.

When *Playboy* found me, or more accurately, when *I* found *Playboy*, I was living at home with my dad, who is a foreman in a steel plant, and my mom, who until recently ran a tiny beauty shop out of our kitchen. Out of four daughters I was the complete dork, the only child in our devoutly Catholic family who wasn't awarded a scholarship to college because of her grades or athletic ability.

(Front) Dad and Mom *(Back, L to R)* Lynette, me, JoJo, and Amy

Perhaps you know me best as the 1994 *Playboy* "Playmate of the Year," or from my role as the zookeeper on MTV's *Singled Out*, or as the girl sitting on the toilet in the ads for Candie's shoes, or as the star of the new NBC sitcom *Jenny*. Whatever.

I'm me. And I still think of myself as a good girl with her dyed roots still firmly planted in the Midwest soil where I grew up. I'm twenty-four years old, and I've only been with five men—each a committed boyfriend, only one connected to show business.

After taking it all off for *Playboy*, I made the cover of seemingly every other magazine in the solar system the old-fashioned way—by working harder than anybody else and hoping, as always, for the best. I had no idea that *Singled Out*, the MTV dating game show, would hit a nerve among Generation Xers not seen since Kurt Cobain plugged in his guitar and sang "Smells Like Teen Spirit." (In truth, my favorite singers are Barry Manilow and Enya. I was never into greasy rocker dudes with drug problems.)

Jenny in Las Vegas, 1996, at Barry Manilow show

That said, I'm not going to pretend that I'm a rocket scientist.

Instead of becoming a campus honey, I was a bratwurst queen who sold sausage sandwiches for minimum wage over the counter at a Polish delicatessen in the same neighborhood where I grew up as a friendless geek. At nineteen, I'd already been turned down by every modeling agency in Chicago as a fat broad with bad hair who'd be lucky to ever get a boyfriend, let alone a career in front of a camera.

Now every time I make the cover of another magazine, I still think of that bitch who worked as the head booker at the largest modeling agency in Chicago, who told me as she put her heel on my metaphorical butt and kicked me out of her office, "You'll never make it in modeling. You look like a barmaid."

Whatever. Bite me.

Now I'm not playing for sympathy. But even though I didn't have money or connections or anybody's faith in me, I always had my soul, my spirit, my family, and my belief that there was going to be more to my life than a job pushing kielbasa-and-onion sandwiches to steelworkers named Belinski.

Still, I was realistic. If I was lucky in this life, I figured back then, I would find a good South Side Chicago blue-collar husband who would help me raise a brood of happy kids inside a little house surrounded by a white picket fence that would keep all of the world's bad karma out, or at least the loathsome peckerheads from my neighborhood from asking me to visit them in the backseat of their beater for a fifteen-minute date. Gentlemen, please!

Somedays now, when I've just been stabbed in the back by another Hollywood scumbag, or by some reporter who's pretended that he's my friend then written stuff about me being a bimbo or a slut that's made my mother cry, I still wonder if that little picket fence is what I should have aimed for.

And yet, back in those not-so-long-ago days when I didn't even place as the most beautiful woman in my family, I used to daydream a lot. After my parents went to bed and our little house was my own, I'd watch TV and fantasize about being in show business. Not famous, just working in front of some camera somewhere.

I never dreamed about being the next Marilyn Monroe or Jayne Mansfield or even Pamela Lee— some big-bosomed chick who turned all the men's heads and who made all the women jealous. Rather, I wanted to be one of my two all-time heroes, Lucille Ball or Carol Burnett. My goal was never to become celebrated for allowing strangers to gaze at magazine pictures of my airbrushed body.

> I NEVER DREAMED ABOUT BEING THE NEXT MARILYN MONROE OR JAYNE MANSFIELD OR EVEN PAMELA LEE—SOME BIG-BOSOMED CHICK WHO TURNED ALL THE MEN'S HEADS AND WHO MADE ALL THE WOMEN JEALOUS.

I wanted, above all else, to make people laugh. I noticed in high school that as long as people were laughing at my goofy jokes or silly faces, they weren't making fun of me, teasing me, calling me bitch or whore or slut, or lying to the world that I'd slept with everybody in the Chicago Bears secondary (I've always preferred men who, in real life, play offense.)

It's been said that show business is just like high school but with money. How true. Indeed, I'm still not sure what made me feel worse about myself—having high school classmates prank-call my mother and tell her that I was screwing every man, boy, and electrical appliance in Chicago, or every other Hollywood producer all of a sudden manufacturing parts featuring nudity when I auditioned for them.

Much more, I told off every Hollywood slime mold who invited me to lie down on his casting couch. Sorry, busters. I know it sounds like naïve bull, but my belief in God, the truth, and that karma—either good or bad—always comes back to you is what got me through those times in Hollywood when all anybody wanted to do was feel me up or throw me down.

There's much more to me than the woman you've seen with the goofy expressions squirting mustard on hot dogs at you on the covers of *Rolling Stone, Newsweek, Playboy,* and *TV Guide.* This is the real me, an open book.

But first a warning to those who've exploited me or screwed with me in the past: Some names will be named, and a few actions will be described in sometimes gruesome

I WANTED TO BE MY TWO ALL TIME HEROES, LUCILLE BALL OR CAROL BURNETT.

and (I hope) hilarious detail. I may be spiritual, but I'm nobody's victim. I'm not out for payback here—I believe in the old Hindu saying, "If you're out for revenge, dig two graves."

But mostly I wrote this book as a record of my life from before and after I went to Hollywood, for the day when I can't remember anymore whether what I remember was really true versus what my press clippings said was true.

It's funny, but one of the things that has marked me as "different" out in Hollywood is that I actually love reading books. Nobody important out here really reads—they usually just hand books and scripts to an underling for a page of "coverage" to explain exactly what is going on in a story.

One item that these clippings haven't picked up on is the fact that I love to read. Now, on those rare occasions when I get a week off, I like nothing better than to find a beach and haul along a suitcase full of books about karma, existence, God, and anything that doesn't have to do with how many Nielsen points one needs to keep his or her television show from getting canceled.

My own book, boys and girls, first tells about my life on a day-to-day basis: the crises, the joys, the tears, me bitching at my boyfriend. You will learn what gives me diarrhea (just about everything.) My life, like this book, is "open"—you can flip to any event in here and read about me without worrying about what came before. It will all make sense.

IMPLANTS/OUTPLANTS
THE BREAST CONFESSION

So how hideously did high school suck? Let me count the ways...

It all began with boobs, and the lack thereof. Like it happens for so many other kids, probably the worst thing that happened to me in high school was that I completely lost whatever sense of self-esteem I'd clung to while growing up and out. In some ways I was lucky that I had no real friends in high school; it's hard to give in to peer pressure when nobody wants to be your peer.

Probably my biggest sense of shame and humiliation came in the shape of my body. Whatever I was, whatever I thought of myself back in high school, I wasn't enough. Why did I have to have zits and stretch marks and moles all over me? Why couldn't I have the perfect bodies that I saw in my boyfriend's copy of *Playboy*?

Anyway, I called my mother in Chicago and told her what I've always considered to be my most shameful secret. "So is there anything in your book that I don't know about?" she asked.

"Well, Mom, uhm, you know, you see," I said, half-stuttering. "I don't know if I'm ready to tell you."

"Oh, no, Jenny, you're scaring me!" she said back.

"Okay, Ma," I said. "Are you sitting down? How do I say this? My boobs? They're saline!"

When I was eighteen and selling sandwiches, I told her, I'd had breast enlargements. It was the biggest secret I'd ever kept from her, and I'd have gone public in the media long before except that I hadn't wanted my mom to know what a dopey, slutty-sounding thing I'd done back when.

"That's it?" my mom said. "You scared me!"

"What do you mean, that's *it*?" I said back.

"Jenny, I knew that, you dummy."

"How, Ma?"

"Well, because your boobs got bigger overnight!"

"Do you care?" I asked.

"No, I just wanted to know why you did it."

With that, for the first time, I actually began trying to figure out why the hell I've always wanted to take those fake boobs out. I've just never experienced that change that I was hoping for that would come with the implants. I thought new boobs would bring perfection, beauty, more self-esteem.

THE OPERATION

My boobs are mostly mine. I used to be between a B and a C cup, which meant, I guess, that I had a perfect handful.

I did the dastardly deed when I was eighteen, at a clinic in Arizona that specialized in doing boob jobs on young girls who didn't want their parents to know what they were up to—and that accepted payment on the installment plan.

My boyfriend at the time was very supportive, as I guess most boyfriends would be when their girlfriends tell them they'd like to have breasts the size of Patriot missiles. So we made up some story to my parents about needing to go to Arizona for vacation and headed south in search of the fountain of boobs.

Anyway, I walked in for my initial consultation and the doctor looked me over as if I were a piece of flank steak. "TAKE YOUR SHIRT OFF!" he commanded me.

Men had been using that line on me for years, but I'd never actually paid someone fifteen hundred bucks for the look-see. I, spying diplomas on the wall suggesting that he'd gotten his license from a medical school where you don't send in your tests by mail, compliantly complied.

The doctor looked me over and, bless his heart, told me the words that would have saved me a lot of dough I could have used back then, as well as the necessity of baring my soul this way in a book that my relatives will read, had I listened to him.

"*What* are you doing here?" the good doctor demanded. "You already *have* breasts. And they're *perky*!"

"I don't care, I don't care, I DON'T CARE!!" I actually yelled at the good doctor, who was trying to give me some sage words of counsel.

Screw "perky," I thought. "Perky" was for loser girls who wanted to be vice president of the glee club. I was a dweeb back then, and I didn't really know how to sing, so, I thought, Screw the glee club too.

Perky boobs might have been fine for Mary Ann on *Gilligan's Island*, but I wanted to be Ginger. I wanted mountains of flesh that would bring the boys running toward me, begging me for dates and my love and the chance to get to know what a great chick I

Perky boobs might have been fine for Mary Ann on *Gilligan's Island*, but I wanted to be Ginger.

was, underneath these fine, monstrous honkers, paid for on the installment plan.

I mean, isn't that the American dream? To purchase fine new breasts on credit?

After figuring out that I wasn't under the influence of major hallucinogens, the doctor proceeded to mark up my perky breasts with a Magic Marker. There were circles and arrows and little grids all over my boobs, making my chest look somewhat like chalkboard diagrams coaches use to outline complicated new plays for their nitwit football players.

Nitwit football players who would soon be mine! (I had already determined that I would reject these turds though, who wouldn't look at me twice when all I had were the perky boobs better left to the fifth-chair cornetists in the marching band.)

After marking up my breasts like some detailed war map, the doctor told me to come back tomorrow for my surgery. My down payment had cleared, so his fit of conscience, I guess, had cleared, too.

That night my boyfriend and I went back to the motel where we were staying and I looked at myself in the mirror, marked up like those pictures of cows you see in butcher shops of the best cuts of beef. The markings, I knew, were where they were going to cut into my flesh and make me a proud product of saline science.

No way, I said. I can't go through with it.

And then I re-reconsidered. I had been so brainwashed into believing that having my boobs blown up to the size of zeppelins would make me instantly secure in the world that I couldn't have been talked out of it had my parish priest come into the operating room and started yelling in my face about the fiery dungeons that awaited me if I went through with it.

I was nervous as hell. When they first get you in the operating room, they shoot you full of Valium so that you'll chill long enough for them to really start to get down to business and begin cutting through the nipples. Anyway, they gave me enough downers to knock out a mule, but still I didn't go down.

> I WOKE UP IN THE MIDDLE OF SURGERY. DON'T YOU HATE WHEN THAT HAPPENS?

So they shot me up again. Finally I was out. Good-bye, Mary Ann. Hello, Ginger. Good-bye, old Jenny, who nobody liked, hello, JENNY, who now everybody would love!

Well, wouldn't you know it, I woke up in the middle of surgery. Don't you hate when that happens? When you look up and there are about thirty-seven different people in gowns holding bloody scalpels over your body?

Before I even saw the blood, however, the first thing I was aware of as I lay on that surgery table was that my arms were spread out and tied down. Let me tell you, for a girl who went to Catholic school for twelve years, a vision like that can keep you in $220-an-hour therapy until the year John-John Kennedy is ready to be president.

Well, of course, I started screaming and crying and kicking to get out of my straps while I lay there on the operating table.

"Give me more drugs!" I screamed, "I'm awake, can't you do something to knock me out?"

"No, Jenny," said someone whose face was behind a mask, "we've already got one done."

And then I could feel this instrument inside my body moving around my new fake breast so that it would fit properly in my chest. That, I could live without. So I kept screaming like a banshee with a harpoon up its butt, and another mask said to me, "It's all right, we're getting there, Jenny."

At that point I felt another surgical instrument inside me, moving the new boob around my innards. By now I was feeling actual organs and tissues being pushed and pulled, so I started bugging out like Jack Nicholson when he was getting electro-shocked in *One Flew Over the Cuckoo's Nest*.

Well, the doctors and nurses had had just about enough of my conniptions, so they called for some huge orderlies, who looked like they played for the Arizona Cardinals, to come and hold me down.

And so the operation that eventually wouldn't hurt my chances to be named Playmate of the Year was finally finished. Ta-daaah!

Ah, but they weren't through with me yet. Some unseen hand pushed a button and suddenly the operating table tilted until I found myself standing up perfectly straight. So there I was, standing with my arms stretched out and my boobs hanging out and still—how shall I put this gently—surgically *open*? It was the most gruesome sight I'd ever seen, with the possible exception of the time I flooded my toilet and dressing room on *Singled Out*.

Meanwhile, across the room, a team of doctors and nurses were standing there scratching their chins and muttering to one another, "I don't know, how do they look to *you*, Doctor?" They were checking on the *hang*.

After much hmmming and intense consultation, they decided that, in yet another case, all that hard studying in medical school had paid off. Jenny had her new boobs.

> I now had the bowling ball–sized breasts I'd always dreamed of. But I felt like I'd just rolled the biggest gutter ball of my life.

They lowered the table, sewed me up, and took me into the recovery room. There, I began projectile vomiting.

I didn't stop throwing up for a week. My boyfriend, Jim, took me back across the street, where I lay in bed and just kept barfing. That time definitely ranks in the top five of gruesome sights I've made, for I was also in the middle of my period and was finding it virtually impossible to make it to the bathroom either to throw up or change my various dressings.

Jim, loyal soldier and boyfriend that he was, cleaned up for me like I was a dog with intestinal worms. The days passed, and I was convinced I'd just made a terrible and ridiculous mistake. The deed was well past done, though, so we eventually checked out of our vomit-flecked motel room and went back to Chicago.

Once home I looked in the mirror and felt disgusted and scarred. My new boobs, I thought, looked horrible. True, I now had the bowling ball–sized breasts I'd always dreamed of. But I felt like I'd just rolled the biggest gutter ball of my life.

I'd been sure that the second I had Marilyn Monroe–sized breasts, I would feel prettier and more secure and everybody in the world would somehow think I was a better person. I was so wrong. I felt just as bad about myself after as I did before.

SO, GIRLS, DON'T DO IT. Not only is the surgery grueling and disgusting, it doesn't really change a thing. Really, I mean it. Wait until you're at least thirty, because then you will have grown up—unlike me at the time I had the operation—and you'll know what's important in life. Then, if you still want them, by all means go for it. But if you grow up and realize that boobs don't mean anything and you don't need the surgery to be beautiful, maybe you'll change your mind.

Now, I know a lot of people out there must think this is a total contradiction, that I must be totally full of it to say that boobs don't make a woman. Sure, I spend all my time *not* trying to play off my breasts.

But would I have been chosen to be Playmate of the Month, and then Playmate of the Year, without my fake boobs? Would I have then moved on to MTV and NBC without these plastic things sewed into my chest?

For God's sake, I'm only twenty-four, I don't have the answers to everything. All I can say for sure is: Take it from me, girls—don't have it done. And guys, take it from me, girls are as obsessed with boobs as you are. For God's sake, breasts make us all feel like *women*, and I don't just mean in a symbolic, breast-feeding way.

That said, I would just like to have them taken out. I've wanted them out ever since I had them in, and now I'm finally going to do it. When they do actually take the implants out of me, they are going to have to stick hoses into my chest just to pump out the saline. Yikes!

At age twenty-four, perhaps I'm finally ready to accept that being Jenny, the *real* Jenny, is, at last, more than good enough.

God, didn't that sound like a winning Miss America speech? If so, is it too late to sign up? And can I go back to being a virgin?

Nope. But I can have them taken out, and I'm going to.

**AT AGE TWENTY-FOUR,
PERHAPS I'M FINALLY READY
TO ACCEPT THAT BEING JENNY,
THE *REAL* JENNY, IS, AT LAST,
MORE THAN GOOD ENOUGH.**

GET OUT OF HELL FREE

Now I myself obviously have a love/hate relationship with getting attention. While I can goof and mug for any camera in the world, I am always stricken with the worst case of stage-fright that anybody I know has ever seen. I'm still not sure why, but I would rather crawl across broken glass in front of an audience of nasty television critics than have to give a speech in public. I freeze. I blank out. I want to crawl under my covers and chant some mantras.

But picking my nose on national television? No problem. That kind of attention I can deal with. In a family, however, it can cause hell when one member is suddenly getting all the notice. Luckily for me I come from a family filled with stars.

Still, sibling rivalry is something we don't talk about in the McCarthy household, especially since the one who so far has gotten the most famous—me—has always, truly, been the loser of the family.

Damn straight. Growing up, I really always thought I would be a nun—maybe a funky nun like Mary Tyler Moore in that Elvis Presley movie *Change of Habit*, or Sally Field in *The Flying Nun*. But a god-fearing nun nonetheless. I wanted to be holy, with a Get Out of Hell Free card, long before I ever wanted to be sexy.

Sex was always something to overcome. In 1995, MTV told my manager, who was then JUST my manager, that they didn't want to audition a *Playboy* Playmate for the *Singled Out* co-host role. "She's smart," he told them, "she's Jenny. You'll understand when you see her."

I REALLY ALWAYS THOUGHT I WOULD BE A NUN—MAYBE A FUNKY NUN LIKE MARY TYLER MOORE IN THAT ELVIS PRESLEY MOVIE *CHANGE OF HABIT*, OR SALLY FIELD IN *THE FLYING NUN*.

512 INTER RUPTIONS A DAY

One day a reporter followed me around the set of MTV's The Jenny McCarthy Show just to see what my minute-to-minute life was like. During the course of that day, he actually counted that I was interrupted from what I was doing 512 times.

Jenny, we need to change or fix your costume (37 times). Jenny, the film crew from *Entertainment Tonight* is ready for the next shot (6 times). Jenny, we need to rehearse, go over your lines, get a promo, get these fifty-three pictures signed for network executives, have you pose on the set with Suzanne Somers (361 times). And then there were the 37 different times I was asked:

WHAT DO YOU THINK OF PAMELA?

Pamela, Pamela, Pamela, I shall go to my grave with people asking me about Pamela Anderson Lee. She's not my arch-enemy, for sure, I just don't think I'd invite her over to my next jammie-party. (I don't consider anybody my arch-enemy, to be honest, except for my uncle in the priesthood who told me I'd burn in hell for posing for *Playboy*.)

But okay, let's not kid ourselves, Pamela and I have got just a touch of history. Most of it, of course, is because my boyfriend Ray used to manage her. We actually started to be friends, when we first met at the Cannes Film Festival.

Anyway, she's at Cannes promoting *Barbed Wire*, and I'm there because I'm with Ray. The only notoriety that I had at that time was as Jenny McCarthy, Playmate of the Year.

Meantime, this is the climax of her career. She's got three million paparazzi snapping her picture outside, she was bigger at that moment than Madonna. The two of us were getting along pretty well at this point; Pamela seemed like a real down-to-earth girl to me.

But then, at this big film-festival party with all the media present, Pamela got a little wild. At one point, she stood up, and pointed her finger at Ray for all the press to see. "See this guy here?" she said, and then pointed to me, "Well, he's f_____g *her*."

Well, everybody's mouth dropped, and Ray told her to knock it off. Soon thereafter, she called Ray and told him I kept jumping in front of her whenever cameras were around. Which was utter bull. Needless to say, I wasn't allowed at any more of her appearances.

I wasn't competition in any way, but she didn't like it. She left Ray's management.

Now, all spring long people have been asking, What did you think of Pamela mocking you on *Saturday Night Live*? To be honest, I didn't mind that I was made fun of on the show—in fact I thought it was pretty damned funny that they had Pamela throwing spears my way.

They say imitation is the highest form of flattery.

Thanks, Pammy.

MEOW!!

THEY SAY IMITATION IS THE HIGHEST FORM OF FLATTERY. THANKS PAMMY.

meow!!

BEDWETTER!!!!

I was frightened of everything as a child, and I was always sure I would die young, or that the world would end tomorrow, or that I would be hit on the head by a falling comet. I used to imagine a *People* magazine cover of me dying at sixteen, or twenty-one, with the headline **Jenny McCarthy: Tragically Dead . . .**

My sister Joanne and I would cuddle together at night and put our rosaries over each other so that if we died that evening we'd go straight to heaven. I used to lie on the couch and watch the television show *Fame*, and just start bawling whenever they reached that lyric "I want to live forever." I was never quite confident I'd make it to the next day.

I've always been a basket case when it came to stress, and I expressed it for seven years by wetting my bed. My friends would make fun of me because I had to have plastic sheets on my bed until I was ten; sleepovers at other kids' houses, of course, were a constant humiliation.

> **MY FRIENDS WOULD MAKE FUN OF ME BECAUSE I HAD TO HAVE PLASTIC SHEETS ON MY BED UNTIL I WAS TEN.**

The weird part was that I wouldn't be asleep when I peed. My eyes would open, I'd pee, and then I'd realize what I'd done. It was like an out-of-body experience. Then, every night, I would go down to our dark basement, which for me was like entering hell, find fresh sheets, and remake the bed. It was horrible. My parents never punished me for the peeing, yet I couldn't stop.

I was also traumatized by the more than one hundred enemas I had to have while growing up because of my digestive problems. I wouldn't poo for weeks, I'd get really high fevers, and finally the doctors would say it was time for my Sunday enema. Hmm.

Over time I went from bedwetting to getting an ulcer. I think it came from my father's drinking. He never hit my mother or any of the kids, but that night every couple of weeks when he'd come home drunk and yelling scared us all. In so many other ways he was a perfect dad—except on those occasional nights when he'd come home yelling and all the kids would run and hide with the lights off in their rooms. Maybe that's why I've always been afraid of the dark.

I would rather crawl across broken glass in front of an audience of nasty television critics than have to give a speech in public.

I FREEZE. I BLANK.

I want to crawl under my covers and chant some mantras.

My dad never really found what he wanted to do in life. His dream had been to own a car wash. Instead, he worked at a steel plant for thirty years, always wishing he had done something else.

He just never learned how to cope with his own issues and secrets. He was one of twelve kids and came from a family with no money. The story of his life was that he went to Vietnam, came home, and married my mom. Within a year, they had their first child. That was it.

Just recently my parents have met with divorce lawyers, which is something they probably should have done twenty years ago. In some ways I've been cheering them on to get divorced for decades, but now that the reality is setting in that this is really going to happen it makes my heart break. No matter what, you want your parents to stay together.

My mom feels that she gave the marriage her all, but she's still depressed because it just wasn't good enough. But she did for that marriage more than any other woman could have done. I recently went to a shrink for the first time, but we didn't really connect and I haven't gone back. What stuck in my craw was that she said after hearing my whole story, "It's about your mother."

It wasn't! My mom was a self-sacrificing woman who did everything she could for her family. Her marriage may have failed, but it taught me for my own relationships that I'm striving for more.

That said, I'm also realistic. I know that no one out there is really Prince Charming. Even if it seems as if somebody has no emotional baggage right now, it always shows up on future flights.

My father, despite his own problems communicating, by example taught me how important it is to get past a roadblock and move on. Though he never got his car wash, I learned by what he didn't do that I should at least chase my own dream.

Seeing him unfulfilled gave me the motivation to do things, like walk through *Playboy*'s doors at a time when I really didn't want to live anymore. And boom—change happened. Courage!

I'm striving for more.

MEET MIKE THE TILE

My way of escaping the stress of growing up in a chaotic household was to make up an imaginary world in the bathroom, where I could be alone with made-up pals. The toilet paper, the shower curtain, the wall were my friends. When I was six, I would sit on the toilet and just *talk* to them.

From the other side of the door my mom would ask, "Who are you speaking to?" And I would call her in and say, "There's Mike the tile, and Tom the toilet paper—he's a new friend."

My grandpa once broke the shower door, and I had a nervous breakdown because to me it felt like a close friend had died. The bathroom was a place to escape into a fantasy world, to escape the stress of our household.

I'd also have long chats in the bathroom with my guardian angels. I never actually saw these angels, but we always had full discussions about why I always peed in bed and my digestive problems, and how I didn't want to go to hell. These conversations with invisible forces were among the most comforting things in my life.

> MY GRANDPA ONCE BROKE THE SHOWER DOOR, AND I HAD A NERVOUS BREAKDOWN BECAUSE TO ME IT FELT LIKE A CLOSE FRIEND HAD DIED.

They say this is how people become creative when they're little. The heartaches of growing up either kill you or make you invent a new way to express your grief. Strong people are resilient and find positive ways to express that stress by becoming creative.

When you're living in a house where there's a lot of chaos, the bathroom is the one place where you can lock the door and escape into a fantasy world, which in a way is what I've done here in Hollywood. I never really go out except to work; it's a great escape from the pain of life. But when I'm alone in the dark again, I have to deal with all the stresses that got me there in the first place.

I'm trying to get better at being alone. Last year I went on a spiritual retreat, where the whole point was to live in a log cabin for seven days with no television or phones. For me, it was like signing up for hell. Ten people were at the retreat at a time, and every day we'd get together for spiritual conversations. The point of my daily talk was about how lonely I was.

One of the main themes of my whole life has been loneliness. In college, I felt like I was so low that I could kill myself, when I felt totally disconnected from everybody and everything in the world.

To this day I can't stand being alone. I rented a house early this year in Beverly Hills, and I haven't slept there in six months. Now I always stay at Ray's, and if he's in another room, I have to have one of my dogs right next to me. I have to go to bed with the television on.

While I can meditate quietly at my Native American sweat lodge every Monday, I can't handle silence at home. I freak out. That's because I was never alone at home growing up. We called our house Grand Central, and I sort of imagine I'll re-create that world a little when I have my own family.

I think I'll get married at about thirty and then pop out three kids right away. All my sisters are only two years apart, and I liked that feeling of closeness that comes from having siblings so close in age.

I've always been terrified of much more than being alone. I'm also scared of ghosts, the dark, burglars, and things that go bump in the night. I've actually *seen* ghosts. Once, when I was in Hawaii with a girlfriend, we were walking in a forest during a full moon and forty ghosts with human faces walked past us. They were dressed as if from the nineteenth century, and I always thought they were people who'd been on a ship that had sunk and were now forever waiting to be rescued.

And no, I wasn't on Maui wowie.

(L to R) Amy, JoJo, Lynette, and me

TO THIS DAY I CAN'T STAND BEING

ALONE.

JFK, JR., AND MY TONGUE

Despite my earlier declarations about not making goofy faces on-camera, I'm still willing to listen if somebody has what he or she thinks is a funny idea. That's why I agreed to have my tongue painted with the American flag for the July cover of *George*, a monthly political magazine edited by John F. Kennedy, Jr.

When I saw the issue for the first time, I had to admit that I liked this cover a lot. With my painted tongue stuck out of my mouth, I looked like Betsy Ross as she might have appeared on a Rolling Stones album cover. Cool!

I also liked the cover line: JENNY McCARTHY on Boris Yeltsin & Pamela Anderson Lee.

I don't think the editors were expecting much out of me beyond a hot cover image to sell their magazine. Still, I tried my best to be smart and funny and to express the real me in the "If I Were President" questionnaire that they sent along for publication with my cover photo.

PEEING NEXT TO FAMOUS PEOPLE: MY NIGHT AT THE OSCARS

I couldn't believe it this spring when a fancy, engraved invitation arrived at my house from the Academy of Motion Picture Arts and Sciences. None of the movies I've had bit parts in did well—anybody remember that blip of me in Tom Arnold's *The Stupids* or me as the nurse to the always charming (not) Christopher Walken in *Things to Do in Denver When You're Dead?*

Knowing all this, I couldn't imagine why the Academy (whatever or whoever that is) would want to make me an honored guest who'd get to walk down the red carpet and sit up close to the stage with the real movie stars.

But then I heard that the Oscar people were trying to hip up the show this year and for once try to appeal to Generation Xers who normally wouldn't make a point to tune

Name Your Party. "Disco Inferno" Your Campaign Song Would Be? "Everybody Must Get Stoned" Why Should We Elect You? Because I'm Not a Real Blonde. Why Shouldn't We? I use too much bleach. What Would Be Your First Act in Office? Wire MTV throughout the White House. Whom Would You Pardon? Eve. Boris Yeltsin is: the ideal drinking partner. In Your Expert Opinion, Which Two Political Figures Should Try Dating? Janet Reno and Hillary Rodham Clinton. As the Leader of the Free World, What Person Would You Model Yourself On? The Dalai Lama. What Would You Fight Hardest to Change? Hunger. What Would Be Hardest to Change? Don King's hairdo. Name a Reason to Go to War: To bring back the McRib sandwich at McDonald's. If You Could Create a New Department, What Would It Be? Collection of All Firearms. What Would Be Your Favorite Presidential Perk? Having all those secrets. What Three Objects Must You Have in the Oval Office? Ashtray, refrigerator, microwave. Bill Clinton Had Bimbo Eruptions. You'll Have... PMS eruptions. Who Would Top Your Lincoln Bedroom Guest List? Pink Floyd. If Your Presidency Were a Sitcom, What Would It Be Called? Jennygate. What Government Agency Would Pamela Anderson Lee Head? Who?

in to the usual Academy Awards snorefest featuring fat, old bald guys with bad rugs giving really long speeches about how thankful they were that Bob Hope gave them their big break.

By the way, who the hell is Bob Hope, anyway? Give me Tom Cruise. *Pleazzze.* And Olivia Newton-John, my idols.

But I digress. Anyway, the Academy wanted me, the unofficial symbol of Gen X, to walk up that red carpet, smile at Army Archerd, and show all the kids at home that the Oscars aren't so lame-o after all.

I'll say! I had a total blast at the Academy Awards, although as usual I embarrassed myself about half a dozen times. The biggest error I made—which every newspaper in the galaxy picked up on—was that I, by mistake, wore my Valentino designer dress backward. I did. I did. I really did. I don't know how that happened, but forty billion people saw me in a zillion-dollar dress that I'd put on the wrong way. Geek à la mode.

No, I wasn't even trying to be goofy old Jenny—I just couldn't tell the front from the back of the dress (it had been a particularly grueling day on the set of *The Jenny McCarthy Show* when I tried it on, and I guess I was distracted).

When Valentino saw me get out of the limousine at the front of the auditorium, he looked as shocked as if I'd popped out wearing a nun's habit. He freaked. All of Hollywood was offering

him their firstborn children in exchange for genuine Valentino creations, and, dork that I am, I put mine on ass-backward.

Well, that's the price you pay when you're a sensitive artist such as myself.

There was celebrity gridlock from the end of the red carpet all the way to the front of the Shrine Auditorium door, so Ray and I just took in the goofy Hollywood carnival that was floating around us. Shoehorned into the crush of sweaty humans in expensive gowns, I finally skipped out of line and instead went over to the grandstand that had been set up alongside the auditorium for fans who'd waited around for a couple days just to get a peek at Mel Gibson's butt or Barbra Streisand's rock.

Personally, I still couldn't believe that *I* wasn't forced to stand on the other side of that grandstand with all the little kids. I'm still not used to being "famous," whatever that means, and whenever I meet a famous person I tend to get all tongue-tied. Either that or start babbling to them nervously and end up sounding like a total retard.

Take what happened when I met Madonna later that night at one of the swanky post-Oscar parties. She was sitting at a table with a group of friends, and I've always loved her, so I just got up the courage and went over to say hello.

"I'm a wallflower tonight," Madonna told me, explaining why she was sitting against the wall.

FORTY BILLION
PEOPLE SAW ME
IN A ZILLION-
DOLLAR DRESS
THAT I'D PUT ON
THE WRONG WAY.
GEEK À LA MODE.

Whenever I meet a famous person I tend to get all tongue-tied. Either that, or start babbling to them nervously and end up sounding like a total retard.

But I was so nervous that I thought she said, "I like the Wallflowers." I thought she meant the band. Well, the Wallflowers had just been on my MTV show, and they've got a huge number one hit record, and I was so excited that Madonna and I had something in common that I started saying, "Me, too! I just love the Wallflowers! Have you heard their new record? That lead singer is HOT!!"

She just stared blankly ahead. I then realized what an ass I'd made of myself and slowly tiptoed away.

So, I screwed up my big chance to chat up Madonna on the meaning of it all. That meant that the best moment of this very weirdly cool night was when I wandered off the runway and red carpet and talked to all the kids and fans in the grandstand. I waved and signed autographs, and all these little girls rushed over to say hi, and that felt the best of all.

I remember how horrible it could be to grow up as a little girl without any real role models, so I like to look out for the little chicks.

I still remember this one little girl who said to me on Oscar night, "I like when you pinch and beat up the boys on *Singled Out*. There's a lot of times I'd like to do that."

A lot of girls say that to me, and it's for them that I always liked to bop the boys on the show. In some small way, I thought each of my punches was a symbolic blow against every boy who's ever teased or tormented a girl on any playground. It happened to me once, too—now take THAT!

Then again, I had no choice but to fight back against the fifty animals I had penned in who wanted a date with the hot chick on that day's episode. It was like I was fighting back for girls everywhere against one giant fifty-headed penis, armed only with my two elbows and my microphone.

(A lot of men also ask me why I was always hitting the boys on the show. Am I a lesbian, some want to know? Go bite yourselves, you fools.)

True, it wasn't always pleasant on *Singled Out*, wading into that sweating, farting mass of testosterone five days a week, but I did learn a lot about human nature, heh-heh. By the end of my time on *Singled Out*, there was only one rule down on the floor—NOBODY TOUCH JENNY. *You* try getting your boobs grabbed on about seventy-four shows in a row, and you'll understand why I made that my only rule.

I wasn't being a prima donna—you just can't imagine how many of those guys liked to pinch my butt while the camera panned elsewhere. All that, for the $300 an episode I got paid! I'm not whining—like the years I hawked Polish sausage, working on *Singled Out* was both an opportunity and a different form of paying my dues.

IT WAS LIKE I WAS FIGHTING BACK FOR GIRLS EVERYWHERE AGAINST ONE GIANT FIFTY-HEADED PENIS, ARMED ONLY WITH MY TWO ELBOWS AND MY MICROPHONE.

For that, I'm forever grateful to MTV. But keep your meathooks off me while I'm working, boys, or you'll find somebody's footprint on your butt.

On Academy Awards night, however, I was hugging everybody like I was some Gen-X Evita—the little kids, the big kids, Army Archerd. I still couldn't believe that the invitation hadn't come to my house by mistake.

I still felt so much closer to the little girl who used to walk around the house surgically attached to her Mr. Microphone than to this sex symbol—Me!—posing for the paparazzi in my backward Valentino dress. (Okay, Valentino? Have I said your name enough now? I've still got this Catholic guilt thing going.)

And then, right before we got to the door of the auditorium, I saw Joan Rivers try-

OKAY, VALENTINO? HAVE I SAID YOUR NAME ENOUGH NOW? I'VE STILL GOT THIS CATHOLIC GUILT THING GOING.

ing to wave me over to the spot where she was reviewing the spectacle for the E! channel. Now, I never knew why, but Joan Rivers has always had it in for me—she's always called me a slut and a bimbo without knowing the first thing about me, so I had no real burning desire to go over to Joan and be humiliated by her again on live national television.

Ray, gentleman that he is, took my arm and firmly walked me around Joan Rivers, who stared daggers at us. All that week, I kept hearing from people how Joan had ripped me for the usual reasons. She said I looked like I'd just stepped out of a whorehouse and that I'd be more than willing to lie down on the red carpet and let every guy look up my dress. Bitch! What if somebody said that about your daughter?

Who cares, right? Except that my mother happened to be watching Joan Rivers and saw that cranky gasbag take me apart. Mom, being Mom, was devastated and started bawling. Nobody hurts my mommy! Personally, I've heard a lot worse. But when somebody like Joan Rivers hurts my mommy, I want to slap the old hag!

Thanks, Joan—I know you've had a tough life and all, and I really do respect the fact that once upon a time you were a great stand-up comedian who broke a lot of new ground for women who wanted to be funny onstage. But did you have to be so f_ _ _ _ _g *mean*?

Take Goldie Hawn, who is one of my all-time favorite comedians and actresses. She's also a major role model, because in a lot of ways she's done what I hope to someday do, in a manner that's allowed her to stay both funny and herself. I've seen some of Goldie's old skits and routines on *Rowan and Martin's Laugh-In*, and I can't believe how terrific, smart, and funny she was back in the days when she was the age I am now.

But there Goldie is on tape, dancing as a

When somebody like Joan Rivers hurts my mommy, I want to slap the old hag!

young ditzy woman in her bikini with "sock it to me" painted on her body...and she's hysterical! I know a lot of people thought Goldie was a bimbo back then, just like a lot of the population thinks I'm an airhead now.

But, God, Goldie sure showed them. And today, *Private Benjamin* is still one of my all-time favorite movies.

So of course Goldie was there at the Academy Awards with Kurt Russell, and I just had to go over and tell her how much she's meant to me and what an inspiration she's been. So I made a point of stopping at her side and of course started babbling nonsensically, because I was so nervous at facing one of my heroes.

Still, Goldie was nice to me. True, she looked at me as if I were some sort of strange creature—I'm still not sure whether she had any idea who, if anybody, I was. But she still seemed really human. She took a moment to *see* me.

And that's all I wanted—to share a moment with her, to say hi, to let her know that all the shit she'd undoubtedly gone through in her career hadn't been in vain. All I really wanted from her was just what all those little girls in the Oscar grandstand wanted from me that night.

Finally, Ray and I made it to our seats, way up front with all the stars. I *still* couldn't believe I was there. Once seated, I loved being there for every second of the forty-seven-hour show. I know it's hip to slag the Oscars, but, hey, it was a hip honor for me to go to the ladies' room and pee next to the famous people I got to pee next to. If you know what I mean.

After the ceremonies were over, but before the big parties, Ray and I drove to a McDonald's drive-through and scarfed some Big Macs, my favorite comfort food. Then it was over to that famous postawards bash held every year by *Vanity Fair* magazine. It's one of the big Hollywood to-die-for parties, meaning that if you weren't invited, you don't really matter in this town and you might as well slit your wrists.

Believe me, I know this scene from the wrong side of the velvet rope. It's funny, but I actually tried to crash the *Vanity Fair* party last year and was turned away (and humiliated!) at the door by some snooty Hollywood bitch with a clipboard, Armani glasses, and the smile of a crocodile. I read her mind that night—what difference did it make, I knew she thought, if she treated me like trailer trash? After all, I wasn't on "the list." I was a NOBODY.

SHE LOOKED AT ME AS IF I WERE SOME SORT OF STRANGE CREATURE—BUT SHE STILL SEEMED REALLY HUMAN. SHE TOOK A MOMENT TO *SEE* ME.

Well, this year we pulled up, got out, approached the door, and there was the self-same Miss Clipboard again, waving people in and calling security on anybody who looked like they were SOMEBODY. Well, lo and behold—this year, I guess I was.

For once, I didn't say anything, just nodded politely as she gushed all over me and kissed my butt and told me I was a greater woman than Mother Teresa and Madame Curie combined.

"JENNY McCARTHY!!" she said, more warmly than my oldest friend in the world. "What a pleasure it is to finally MEET you!"

Bite me.

One of the most interesting encounters I had at the party was with Courtney Love, whom I'd never met but who raced across the floor to greet me like I was her long-lost soul sister. I didn't know quite what to expect from her—she was all glammed out as the "new" Courtney, but I'd heard the usual stories and read the same old articles about how she was the ultimate psychobitch from hell.

But Courtney was certainly very nice to me. "You rock, Jenny McCarthy!" she yelled as she embraced me. "You're a f _ _ _ _ _ g feminist!"

> Courtney was certainly very nice to me. "You rock, Jenny McCarthy!" she yelled as she embraced me. "You're a f _ _ _ _ _ g feminist!"

At first, I was kind of taken aback. Back where I grew up, in blue-collar, rigidly Catholic Chicago, the word *feminist* was kind of considered to be a negative thing. "Feminists," I grew up believing, were women who were dykes, or who didn't shave their legs, or who didn't like it when other women had any fun. An enlightened place, yes?

I love Courtney. I've since run into her at a few parties, and she reminds me of me. She's a risk taker and doesn't give a shit what other people think.

DIE, BITCH

It's no secret that I'm a competitive chick. I'm always worried about the next up-and-coming version of whatever I'm doing. My spiritual side says, "No, we *need* people to be up and coming," but the nonspiritual side of me says, "Die, bitch." That was one of the reasons it wasn't easy to pass the baton on to Carmen Electra when I was through with *Singled Out*.

I got my competitiveness from my parents, who put all their daughters in every sport that was available for girls on the South Side of Chicago. I always won the fifty-yard dash at the park races, and I always needed to be Most Valuable Player, no matter what I was doing. My ambition is always in turbo gear; even if I'm exhausted, I can't stop revving.

It never stops. As soon as I signed on the dotted line for the first time with *Playboy*, I immediately said, "I have to be Playmate of the Year." The funny thing is that I didn't win in the readers' poll—that was Miss Hot Wax December Poon Girl. Rather, I was named Playmate of the Year because so many people who worked for *Playboy* wrote Hugh Hefner and told him how hard I'd worked as Miss October. For a full year I was never late, talked to everybody at every party, and tried to work hard. And it worked.

At the same time, I don't feel my competitiveness comes out viciously. I just leave the feeling inside me, say to myself, "I'll do it, I'll do it"—and then I wait for my trophy.

So many of the other Playmates have gone the *Playboy* route because they were either sexually abused when they were young or were getting back at their boyfriends. I didn't fall into either of those categories.

It was my way out of a hard, lonely situation, the same way talking to the bathroom tiles was my way out when I was five years old. Now all I try to do is plan one year ahead. When I was at *Playboy* I said, "I want to work for MTV" and seven months later I auditioned and got the part on *Singled Out*.

And then I said I wanted my own television show, and that happened too. Now I want to do a really special movie. At fifty, I want to be Goldie Hawn or Tom Hanks, spreading good, funny stuff. No evil Faye Dunaway roles yelling "Christina!!" while waving a wire hanger for me!

And then, when I'm sixty or seventy and the kids are out of the house and my husband dies, maybe I'll teach or be a nurse. I'll probably still be afraid to be alone, so I'll have to mix it up with as many people as I can.

Me and co-star Heather Paige Kent

I ACTUALLY TRIED TO CRASH THE *VANITY FAIR* PARTY LAST YEAR AND WAS TURNED AWAY (AND HUMILIATED!) AT THE DOOR BY SOME SNOOTY HOLLYWOOD BITCH WITH A CLIPBOARD, ARMANI GLASSES, AND THE SMILE OF A CROCODILE. WELL, THIS YEAR WE PULLED UP, GOT OUT, APPROACHED THE DOOR, AND THERE WAS THE SELF-SAME MISS CLIPBOARD AGAIN, WAVING PEOPLE IN AND CALLING SECURITY ON ANYBODY WHO LOOKED LIKE THEY WERE SOMEBODY. WELL, LO AND BEHOLD—THIS YEAR, I GUESS I WAS. "JENNY McCARTHY!!" SHE SAID, MORE WARMLY THAN MY OLDEST FRIEND IN THE WORLD. "WHAT A PLEASURE IT IS TO FINALLY MEET YOU!"

BITE ME

my
obsession

with
digestion

I know it sounds tacky that my first priority on the night that I attended the most exclusive show in the world was to get to a McDonald's drive-through window so I could inhale a Big Mac. I know, I know, I'm a celebrity now; I'm supposed to send somebody out to pick me up some Beverly Hills blackened catfish or Senegalese caviar or whatever it is that Wolfgang Puck or *Entertainment Tonight* say celebrities are supposed to eat.

(*Previous spread*) Here I am, a sophomore in high school, eating like a pig

'Tain't me. When I'm hungry, I've got to eat. Lots, preferably via a drive-through. And NOW!

I guess I've always been that way about food. My parents have always said that I was the easiest of the four girls when we were little. I was one of those smiling, blond Hallmark Card kind of babies who always just seemed happy to be breathing on the planet. Except, that is, when I was hungry.

Then I would scream and yowl like Joan Jett in concert on the night of her worst PMS ever. I was like that big goofy plant, Audrey II, in *Little Shop of Horrors*, who when she was hungry would vacuum anything, everything, and everybody in sight into her mouth.

My folks actually have home-movie footage of me as a baby showing what a pig I was. Because I was so fat and loved food so much, my parents had to feed me together. I'd be sitting in my high chair, and my mother would begin by spoon-feeding me some baby goo. My dad, meanwhile, had to be immediately ready with a second spoonful because I'd start shrieking for more the moment I'd swallowed the first.

By the time I was in grammar school, teachers had already noticed my less-than-delicate palate. Believe it or not, it was a teacher at my Catholic school who gave me my first nickname, and it stuck to me until the year I got my first training bra. For years, I was called "Truck Driver"—because I ate like one.

Not real nice, but I understood at least where it came from. There I'd be in third grade, sitting in the lunchroom, and everybody would watch as I'd take out three or four peanut-butter-and-jelly sandwiches, plus enough potato chips and Chips Ahoy to feed the Turkish navy, which my mother had packed for me the night before.

And then, before their eyes, I would chow down so fast and furiously that people actually thought I was some kind of hunger-crazed mutant. "Food! Food! Food!" I shrieked, and they just kept shoving it in.

> FOR YEARS, I WAS CALLED "TRUCK DRIVER" —BECAUSE I ATE LIKE ONE.

But "Truck Driver" wasn't so bad. It was a whole lot better than the nickname those bitches in high school gave me. To them I was "Barbie," as in the doll. Tell me about how Hollywood is the meanest place in the world—try high school!

Being a little kid was a lot easier. Even then, I guess, I dreamed about one day being a star. My very first memory of being alive is taking a crayon and writing my name really big on my mother's living-room wall. I guess I was born wanting to see my name in lights, but boy, did I get my butt beaten for that one!

I was one of those sm
Card kind of babies w
happy to be breathing

Except, that is, when I was...

Me, age 3

ing, blond Hallmark
o always just seemed
on the planet.

hungry.

It's weird how you can be a person who is both totally shy and exhibitionistic. I'm not sure if it was a foreshadowing of what was to come, but I remember being four years old and going to church with my mom, as we kids did every single Sunday. This particular Sunday, however, I'd neglected to put on underwear, a fact my mother didn't catch as she herded us out that day.

After the service, I got separated from my family, and I remember hearing my mother walking up and down the aisles, going, "Jenny, Jenny, where are you?"

She finally found me sitting in a pew in my little frilly white dress. Except I was sitting there with no underwear on and my legs spread like I was in a gynecologist's stirrups. What a charming four-year-old you have, Mrs. McCarthy!

I only remember one other time that I was able to get out of the house and to church without my mother knowing I didn't have any underwear on. It was a few weeks after I'd struck my innocent pose in the church pew.

This time, I decided to make my statement in the middle of mass. I remember that everyone was listening to the homily when I started rubbing my bare butt cheeks against the wooden pew because I liked the squeaky sound emitted by butt against board.

The service just ground to a halt and everybody in the parish went, "Oh, my God, what is that?"

My mother, bless her soul, just looked at me and said, "Jenny, you didn't wear underwear again, did you?"

Sorry, Mom.

BUT "TRUCK DRIVER" WASN'T SO BAD. IT WAS A WHOLE LOT BETTER THAN THE NICKNAME THOSE BITCHES IN HIGH SCHOOL GAVE ME. TO THEM I WAS "BARBIE," AS IN THE DOLL. TELL ME ABOUT HOW HOLLYWOOD IS THE MEANEST PLACE IN THE WORLD—TRY HIGH SCHOOL!

I rely on the Jenny McCarthy Stress Diet to stay thin in Hollywood. When I first moved out here, I weighed 140 pounds. I was very happy at that weight, but everyone said I had to slim down because in Hollywood you had to be skinny. So every single day I dutifully drank two gallons of water, took two step classes, and ate nothing but boiled chicken and broccoli, just like you're supposed to.

I felt great physically, but I was depressed as hell. So I started eating again like I did at home in Chicago, relying on Taco Bell and Big Macs. Back home I couldn't eat that way and stay in shape, but with all the stress out here, I manage to keep the weight off.

Anorexia was never my eating disorder—rather, I liked to graze all day like a cow. I don't have normal bowel movements anymore, they're all diarrhea. Obviously, running to the bathroom four times a day is not the healthy way to stay in shape, and my butt sure is sore. But when you're so stressed out from working seventeen hours a day, every day, it works.

Sadly, there's no easy diet plan for girls—it's all about exercise. If you love food, then you simply have to do it. I just started with a personal trainer, went twice, and fractured my foot. So we'll see if I can practice what I preach.

BAD BOYS

When I think of teenage boys, all I can remember is the cruelty of the cool ones. I would like to say to all of them: Don't be such jerks! Be yourself and treat the girls with a little respect. Write a love letter to a girl instead of just trying to get one to grab your pee-pee. (That goes for older men, too. I still think there's nothing more romantic than a love letter.)

I think women are *always* much more mature than men. When I was thirteen, my boyfriends acted like they were seven. It seemed like the only boys who wanted the fairy tale to be true about how ladies and gentlemen should treat each other were the quiet, geeky guys. All the cool fellows in seventh grade were the assholes who were going around telling everybody that "Jenny McCarthy French-kisses like a lizard!"

That was not cool. It hurts like a thousand daggers when you're twelve and your

1 McDONALD'S

I still haven't emotionally recovered from the loss of the McRib sandwich. Is there a twelve-step support group for those of us in recovery from the McRib? If not, I may have to kill myself.

2 TACO BELL

"Run for the border," they say, and that's what I do whenever possible, for the Taco Supremes, and the Taco Supremes only. I'm a very loyal gal. Then I run to the toilet, which has nothing to do with the fine cuisine served up here, but with the delicate nature of my digestive tract. Even if I'm at Ma Maison, the first thing I look for is the location of the bathroom, not the list of the appetizers.

My Five Favorite

FAST FOODS

3 BURGER KING

I would be honored, always, to be the queen between your buns. My army for a Whopper with Cheese.

4 WHITE CASTLE

You may have to be from the Midwest to understand the deep inner meaning of a White Castle slider square hamburger, but let me tell you, they taste fabulous sliding right in—and they come out the other end just as smoothly.

5 ANY HOT DOG JOINT

Any hot dog joint at all. As they used to say about Patty Duke on her old sitcom, a hot dog just makes me lose control.

boyfriend breaks up with you because he thinks you're a geek. Those were the exact words I heard. I was a geek. Good-bye.

The worst part of all this is that every girl has to make her own mistakes on the road to being with a good guy. People can tell you what to do, but you won't listen when you're growing up. As soon as my mom said "Don't date that guy," I knew I was going to go right ahead and see that very person.

Take Rodney Hendricks, who gave me thirteen hickeys on my neck in seventh grade before I even knew what a hickey was. I was so innocent and trusting, and the next day I had to go Catholic school with Cover Girl makeup on my neck. All the boys called me "slut" and I didn't even *know* what a hickey was. That's when I began to lose my innocence: at the very point where you learn you can't always trust what people say or do.

I WAS A GEEK.
GOOD-BYE.

Yet in some ways I loved Rodney even more for being so evil. He was a challenge. Girls are like that; it can be hard to like a man who is always kissing your ass, because they're just too easy. Over time, I found I like a man in the middle—someone who will be real, and honest, and respectful, but also not take my bullshit. I think I found that in Ray.

MISS LAYPECK, DID ANYONE EVER DROP YOU AS A BABY?

I never really thought I was pretty growing up. So, even as a tiny kid, I always aimed instead for that very special kind of attention and rush you get from making people laugh. I even went so far as to make a comic scene on my very first morning of kindergarten.

Since it was such a momentous day for everybody, all the kids' moms were allowed to come into the school and our kindergarten class and make sure that all was happy and well. Everybody's dad, needless to say, was at work.

Our kindergarten teacher's name was Miss Laypeck, and as all the mothers sat there with their squirrely kids, I, for some reason, was feeling so comfortable that I found it within me to raise my hand and tell a joke.

"Yes, Jenny?" Miss Laypeck asked.

"Miss Laypeck," I said, really innocently, "did anyone ever drop you when you were a baby?"

"Why, no," she said. "Why do you ask?"

"Well," I said, "if you weren't dropped as a baby, how come you have a crack in your butt?"

All the mothers lost it, and even Miss Laypeck and my mother began turning blue trying to suppress their laughter. That felt great, to get a whole room full of strangers going.

Not all of my comedy at the time, however, was of the same nature as these witty one-liners. Unintentionally, I was also beginning to understand the magic power of physical comedy.

It was story time in kindergarten one day, and I was just sitting there listening to Miss Laypeck read us the tale of some bear family trying to make a happy life for itself in the woods. I remember that I was fiddling with the buckle on my frilly white dress when, all of a sudden, the quiet of the room was pierced by the sound of a tremendous fart.

Well, of course it was me. The entire classroom exploded in chaos, and all the little kids were pointing at one another, trying to figure out who cut the cheese. I was right there with them, pointing to the boy next to me and yelling, "He did it!"

And that, I guess, is where it all began, my obsession with digestion. Hey, it got me on the cover of *Rolling Stone*, no?

MISS DERKAP, PLEASE CAN I USE THE BATHROOM?

Despite the fact that I had a need growing up to occasionally act out in public, I was almost always so intimidated and frightened

of getting up in front of the class and making a spectacle of myself that I would just sit in the back like some speechless dork. Sometimes the results of my almost pathological shyness were disastrous.

Once, in first grade, I remember I really, really had to go to the bathroom. I always had digestive problems when I was little. But I was always superembarrassed about my stomach and kidney problems and always just pretended nothing was wrong.

Anyway, there I was in mean Miss Derkap's first-grade class, and suddenly my stomach started yowling. "Miss Derkap," I said, shyly raising my hand, "I really need to use the bathroom."

But she would have none of that. "No, no, Jenny," she told me, "not until you finish all your work."

So I sat there, trying to finish my work as fast as I could. But then, well...I actually pooed in my pants. It just started coming out, and I couldn't control it. I was so embarrassed, because I knew the kids sitting next to me were about to smell it, and I suddenly imagined myself having to change my name and move to another city to escape the shame.

So I raised my hand again and asked Miss Derkap, "Please, please, please, can I use the bathroom?"

"No, Jenny," she said, "not until you finish all your work."

Finally, an hour later, she gave me permission to go to the bathroom. I remember getting up from my seat and walking out of the classroom backward so that nobody would see the big poo stain on the back of my uniform. The horror, the horror!

MISS BONOMO, MR. MICROPHONE, AND ME

There was only one teacher who could ever get me out of my little-girl shell, and that was Miss Bonomo.

She was my second-grade teacher, and I loved her like no other teacher I've ever had. It was her first time teaching, and she really went out of her way to make sure every child in the class felt special. She was the only teacher I ever had who made me want to get up in front of the class every day and talk.

My favorite time in her class was "show and tell"; every single day I'd bring in this Donny and Marie Osmond–endorsed "Mr. Microphone" that you could use to project your voice through a radio just like a real star. Every day I'd start "show and tell" by giving the class a play-by-play over the microphone of what people had brought in that morning.

The reason I was able to make this bold show business–like move to center stage was the support of Miss Bonomo. She always encouraged me to talk and was the only person who ever really gave me the confidence to speak in front of a crowd. Even now, if I'm feeling really phobic or intimidated about talking in front of an audience, I'll think of Miss Bonomo, and somehow I get through it all okay.

Although everyone else probably thought I was retarded, Miss Bonomo understood the importance to me of my Mr. Microphone. It was both my security blanket and magic wand, and when I was holding it, I was able to become another person who wasn't so shy and frightened and lonely. If you asked my mom, all I did my entire childhood was talk into that stupid microphone with the silver ball on top.

When I was little, I would take my older sister Lynette down into the basement and we'd put together these little shows with the help of Mr. Microphone. We'd set up a nice background of plants, dim the lights, and practice some goofy routines for weeks.

Then we'd try to get the whole neighborhood to come over and see

> **EVERY DAY I'D START "SHOW AND TELL" BY GIVING THE CLASS A PLAY-BY-PLAY OVER THE MICROPHONE OF WHAT PEOPLE HAD BROUGHT IN THAT MORNING.**

what we'd come up with. But no one ever came. Unlike kids who spent their childhoods playing board games, I busied myself putting on shows that nobody wanted to see.

We even made a home movie once called *The Revenge of the Pizza Cutter Killer*, starring me, Lynette, and our sister Amy. Lynette was the killer as well as the cameraman, so all you ever saw of her was her hand, holding a pizza cutter, chasing us around the house.

The plot was very avant-garde: Lynette basically just chopped us all up, using ketchup for blood and cheese for guts. We taped some Atari music for a sound track and even made up cue cards. It was all really cool. Thanks to Miss Bonomo, I'm ready for my close-up now, Mr. DeMille!

CA-CHING

After my Donny and Marie microphone, my other favorite plaything growing up was without question a toy cash register that my mother bought me for Christmas one year when I was about seven, after I'd begged her for months. It cost about sixty dollars, which my mother totally scrimped and saved for out of change she'd scraped from the bottom of her purse. Thanks, Mommy!

As soon as I got the cash register, I was permanently obsessed. Looking back, I now realize that a large chunk of my childhood was spent in our basement playing with the cash register buttons and making that *ca-ching!* sound. I would spend hours doing nothing but taking in pretend money and giving out pretend change, and I got really good at playing that machine like a finely tuned instrument.

Years later, when I was a teenager hawking fresh-ground bratwurst at the local Polish deli, I still loved playing with cash register buttons. I'm sure that's why I lasted so many years working at the deli—I just never got tired of making that *ca-ching* noise.

THANKS TO MISS
BONOMO, I'M READY
FOR MY CLOSE-UP
NOW, MR. DEMILLE!

"Miss Larypeck'

innocently, "did

you when you we

no," she said. "U

"Well," I said

dropped as a bab

have a crack in

' I said, really anyone ever drop e a baby?" "Why, hy do you ask?" ". if you weren't r, how come you your butt?"

First grade

D O N ' T   S M O K E :
T H E   J E N N Y   M c C A R T H Y   S T O R Y

Growing up, the only things I loved more than my family were my neighborhood and my block in Chicago. Our street was real lower middle class and cute, in an *All in the Family* kind of way.

Tons of little houses filled with breeding Catholics were shoehorned right next to one another, and since nobody practiced birth control, there seemed to be literally hundreds of little kids to play with right outside my front door.

Every family also seemed to have a dog or two, so it was always complete and utter bedlam on our block. Every spring and summer there would be big block parties and those were some of the best times of all.

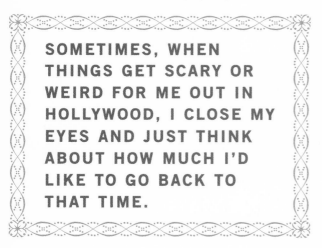

SOMETIMES, WHEN THINGS GET SCARY OR WEIRD FOR ME OUT IN HOLLYWOOD, I CLOSE MY EYES AND JUST THINK ABOUT HOW MUCH I'D LIKE TO GO BACK TO THAT TIME.

I know that the whole idea of a block party sounds so cheesy now, but there was something so cool about an entire community getting together to party, celebrating that the neighborhood had made it through another year. It kind of felt like being alive inside one of those 1950s pictorial stories in *Life* magazine about the American Dream that I sometimes see when I'm browsing in used bookstores.

On hot summer days on my block, someone would always open a fire hydrant. While kids splashed around, mothers clucked to one another from these circles made up of baby strollers. A few yards away children played hopscotch on the sidewalk, while others played baseball or kickball down the street.

As I think back, it reminds me a little bit of living in a wonderful fairy tale. Sometimes, when things get scary or weird for me out in Hollywood, I close my eyes and just think about how much I'd like to go back to that time. Life felt safe back then and really, really fun. And there were no bills!

Chicago has always been justifiably famous for its softball, and I remember playing the game virtually every second that there wasn't snow on the ground. I played twelve-

Our street was real lower middle class and cute, in an **"All in the Family"** kind of way.

inch and sixteen-inch softball, and I really was damn good. Now those memories of playing softball as a little kid are some of my warmest mental pictures.

I played every position. And in a lot of ways I don't think I was ever happier than in those days when I was pitching or playing shortstop or catcher, in front of the entire neighborhood. Getting a hit was the finest preadolescent high I'd ever experienced. God, I miss that part of my life.

During the winter, one of my favorite things to do growing up in the neighborhood was "skeech." It was our blue-collar way of skiing. Chicago, of course, is totally flat, so even if we'd had the dough to buy ski equipment we'd have had to drive for hours in order to find some reasonable hills to ski down.

Instead of that, we "skeeched." Everyone in the neighborhood would wait for a speeding car to go by, then we'd jump on the back and ski all the way down the street until we'd finally let go and jump back into the street. I don't recommend this to anybody, but that's what we'd do for winter fun in Chicago. If I do say so myself, I was a damn good skeecher.

I really don't think I'm romanticizing how I grew up. I mean, the neighborhood I was raised in was a typical, tough, blue-collar part of Chicago where you naturally learned how to fight.

I've always kind of wondered if maybe it's because of my old neighborhood that I beat up so many guys on *Singled Out*. I was just so used to beating up (and getting beat up) as a kid that perhaps I continued it on camera when I grew up.

God, if there's anything I could take back from those days it would be the decision I made in eighth grade to start smoking cigarettes just because all the cool girls did.

Of course, you grow up fast in that kind of tough environment. Everyone in the neighborhood is drinking and smoking cigarettes at an early age, so unless you wanted to be thought of as a total wimp you followed along.

God, if there's anything I could take back from those days it would be the decision I made in eighth grade to start smoking cigarettes just because all the cool girls did. I wanted nothing more in life than to be one of the cool girls. Man, I'm still paying the price for that particular choice.

I keep quitting and starting, quitting and starting. Cigarettes have always been, like, this huge monkey on my back and they've turned into one of the big battles of my life. The part I hate most about smoking cigarettes (besides them killing you and making you smell like a tar pit) is that you can start behaving exactly like any other kind of addict.

Don't Smoke:

The Jenny McCarthy Story

I'll quit smoking for quite a while and then I'll say, "See I can quit, I don't have a problem."

And then I'll have a bad day at work, and I'll think, Oh, just one cigarette won't hurt. And then, within fifteen minutes, I'm hooked again. I know I'm going to kick it once and for all very soon, but it really is a day-by-day process.

So, kids, if you ever have any doubt about whether or not you want to pick up a cigarette, listen to me: DON'T. I'm not just saying this. DON'T. I'm so filled with shame about this topic that there's a part of me that thinks I should name this book *Don't Smoke: The Jenny McCarthy Story.*

I mean it, ya big geeks.

THE NEIGHBORHOOD

Even though I knew how to fight and smoke cigarettes from an early age, this isn't meant to imply that I was a bad girl growing up. No way!

I'm flirting with boys, age 13

I never, ever, went through a shoplifting phase, because I was too frightened of the eternal consequences. Being brought up in a really strict Catholic house scared me into believing that if I ever stole anything I would immediately be launched on a rocketship to hell, where the Devil himself would flog me into eternity. Yikes!

And I hated pot. Yuck! I still remember going to my first concert when I was in sixth grade. It was a Rod Stewart show at some huge stadium and I remember sitting in the very last row thinking that this was the worst music I'd ever heard. And then the people in front of me lit up some reefer and I thought the smell alone would kill me. The whole experience sucked.

Like most of the teenage kids in my neighborhood, however, I drank a little. It was just what you did. If you didn't at least take a sip of something every once in a while, you were a freak. So naturally, when we were fourteen, some girlfriends and I got ridiculous fake IDs from some kids who lived in a bad neighborhood.

I still laugh when I remember the first time the bunch of us all went out on the town with our little plastic cards, which we were sure would grant us entry into every hip place in Chicago. The first joint we went to was a dance club about a half hour south of Chicago called the Crazy Rock.

Now remember, I was fourteen years old with basically no boobs. And of course I was wearing this skintight shirt that I thought was really hot which I wore off my shoulder like some funky older chick. So we all casually strolled into the Crazy Rock club, each of us wearing several metric tons of makeup and hairspray to keep our big, big hairdos in one piece.

Well of course the bouncer came right over to our gang of doofuses and demanded some ID. So we all pulled out our ridiculous new fake identities, and he just looked at all the pictures and fake birthdays and laughed in our faces.

BLONDIE WAS ONE OF THOSE CLASSIC CRANKS ON EVERY KID IN THE WORLD'S BLOCK WHO WOULD GO ABSOLUTELY BAT-SHIT IF ANYBODY STEPPED ON THE TINY PATCH OF LAWN IN FRONT OF HER TINY LITTLE HOUSE.

As things turned out, the bouncer thought we were all so adorable that he just let us in. So there we all were, boogying all night long and drinking our little beers. Fun place, the Crazy Rock, but now it's a strip club.

Yet despite all the neighborhood peer pressure, I can't help but feel fondly about those days when nobody had any money and personal relations just seemed a whole lot easier. Even the neighborhood cranks from back then seem hilarious in retrospect.

Most memorably, there was this one older demented soul down the block who everybody called Blondie. Now Blondie was one of those classic cranks on every kid in the world's block who would go absolutely bat-shit if anybody stepped on the tiny patch of lawn in front of her tiny little house.

Sometimes, we couldn't help it, my friends and I would sit across the street from Blondie's just to watch the daily fireworks. It was just so funny when Blondie came running out of the house in her bathrobe and curlers, screaming at the older kids about how she was going to kill anybody who would dare despoil her teeny little garden of Eden.

"jenny,

you didn't wear
underwear again,
did you?"

SO

RRY,
mom

Once, while hanging out across the street with a few of my little girlfriends, I finally worked up the courage to actually put my foot on Blondie's lawn. Well, of course in two milliseconds out came Blondie yelling that the gates of hell would soon be opening for me. My pals, naturally, all scrammed away so fast you'd have thought they were making a prison break (several of them probably since have).

I've never been so frightened in my entire life as on the day I thought Blondie was going to kill me on her lawn and send me to hell.

I, however, was so frightened by the horrifying sights and sounds of Blondie on the rampage that I froze on her precious lawn. She was shrieking like a banshee, and I was so terrified that I was physically paralyzed. Suddenly, pee started rolling down my leg, and to this day I swear I've never been so frightened in my entire life as on the day I thought Blondie was going to kill me on her lawn and send me to hell.

She's dead now. I wonder if Blondie herself is spending eternity living upstairs or down.

Then, one day when I was little, I was sitting on our front porch and I noticed a man across the street whose pants were down and who was playing with another kind of hose that I was completely unfamiliar with. I was sure he was figuring out some new way to water the grass, but he was really yanking his wanky. Whoah! Daddy!

And he wasn't the only one. When I was growing up, seven different guys jerked off in front of me. The first time it happened, it looked to me as if he was rolling bologna down there, and then I got scared. Living in a house full of girls, I had never seen a penis before.

Even in the most normal-looking neighborhoods you couldn't be too careful. The fact that it was so common is disturbing, but after the first shock it didn't faze me anymore. The last time it happened I was thirteen, walking home from cheerleading practice with my girlfriend, when we saw another guy doing it. Instead of running, we just laughed at him.

EAR PUNCHERS AND DENTAL FEAR

Even as a little kid I was always concerned with fashion and trying to fit in with what was hip. Even then I was usually

My first vacation in Florida, age 10

pretty good at causing totally embarrassing (and usually unintentional) scenes. I still remember the stir I caused in fourth grade when I went to this place called Clara's Boutique in our local mall to get my ears pierced.

My mom came with me and paid the five dollars, but as soon as the ear puncher put the alcohol on my ears I totally freaked out. She held me down and quickly zapped my ear with her gun at which point I fainted. I was lying comatose on the floor in this funky mall store, and the powers-that-be decided that as long as I was already out cold they might as well pierce the other ear, too.

That was my first fashion statement: sprawled out unconscious on the floor of this boutique as I'm straddled by a piercer with a gun. How we women have to suffer to look good!

In fact, unconsciousness was often my first line of defense when faced with new and unknown forms of pain. When I was in kindergarten, my mother dragged me to the dentist because she knew I already had, like, four cavities. I started bawling the second I hit the dentist's chair and started screaming, "I don't wanna, pleeeeze, I just don't wanna."

The dentist was not exactly George Clooney with his bedside manner. "Listen," he told me sternly. "if I don't fill your teeth now, then you're going to have to come back here and I'll pull all of your teeth out of your head."

What a charming thing to say to a kindergartner on her first trip to the dentist! Needless to say, I got even more terrified and shrieked like Courtney Love all through the appointment.

THAT WAS MY FIRST FASHION STATEMENT: SPRAWLED OUT UNCONSCIOUS ON THE FLOOR OF THIS BOUTIQUE AS I'M STRADDLED BY A PIERCER WITH A GUN.

From that day on, I've always been afraid to go to the dentist. When I got a little older, my biggest fear was that they were going to knock me out with gas and start fondling my boobs. Actually, I'm still afraid that dentists are going to do that. So now I always make sure there's a woman dental technician in the room, if I've got to get knocked out. Girls can't be too careful these days.

MY IDOLS: WONDER WOMAN AND OLIVIA NEWTON-JOHN

Like most little girls, I had tons of heroes growing up. My first big idol was Lynda Carter as Wonder Woman. It wasn't her acting that got me so excited; it was just the idea of this woman who could conquer the world for the forces of good with her superpowers. I always loved that kind of magic.

God, I always thought, if only I could have superpowers too and solve all the world's problems, including how

MY FIRST BIG IDOL WAS LYNDA CARTER AS WONDER WOMAN.

to get my family more money so life wouldn't be such a struggle for my folks. Thinking Lynda Carter might have some answers for me, I used to write to Wonder Woman once a month when I was a little kid.

I'd write her these dorky letters begging her to give me some wisdom, her costume, or maybe just an autographed picture. I waited and waited, and ran to the mailbox each day to see if Wonder Woman had written back. But I never once got a response.

Naturally, I was heartbroken. I've always remembered that incident, which is why I always try to respond to as much fan mail as I can. I know what it feels like to be little and want a picture of your hero so badly that you could die—and then to come out with nothing. It's a terrible feeling. As they say, show business isn't dog-eat-dog. It's dog-doesn't-return-other-dog's-phone-calls.

I got much luckier with Olivia Newton-John, my second big childhood hero. I was so happy when I got a signed 8 x 10 picture from her in the mail because she was just so sexy, beautiful, and could sing like nobody I'd ever heard.

Olivia Newton-John *was* Sandra Dee, in my mind, and that's who I wanted to be, too.

I was still a little girl, but it was also right around that time that I

Olivia Newton-John *was* Sandra Dee, in my mind, and that's who I wanted to be too.

(Top) Me, age 6, with my Olivia Newton-John hairdo
(Right) Sandra Dee remake for MTV with Idalis as Rizzo

decided that before I became a world-famous movie star I would first be a world-famous rock star. Some girlfriends and I even made up our own band. We didn't have a name for the group, but we had little fake drums, a guitar, and an organ that we'd goof around on and write our own songs. We were basically trying to imitate the Go-Go's, the girl band that had that number one record "We Got the Beat" in the early 1980s.

I even put on a little rock show once with my sister Lynette and another little girl who lived down the block. Our next-door neighbors were having a picnic one day in their backyard, and we all went over and announced that we were going to sing a song that we'd written especially for the occasion.

After getting everybody's attention, we three stood there and sang this song with lyrics that went, "It's Saturday night/and I want to start a fight/I'm really in the mood/to start a fight."

We really liked the song, but no one clapped. That was the last time I really dreamed about being a rock star.

MY CRUSHES: MISTER ROGERS, SCOTT BAIO, AND ERIK ESTRADA

And of course there were always boys and men whom I idolized when I was growing up. Embarrassing as it is to say, my first major crush was on Mister Rogers.

I was totally addicted to *Mister Rogers' Neighborhood*, and every day after school Lynette and I would get into these huge fights in front of the television about whether she or I was the girl who would eventually get to marry him. It wasn't until I was grown up that I realized what a dork his character really was.

Then came my equally unfortunate Chad Lowe phase. Chad, if you don't remember, was a teenybopper idol of the second whose longest-lasting claim to fame is that he's Rob Lowe's younger brother. He was the blond version of Rob Lowe and I used to cut out pictures of him and Ricky Schroeder from teen magazines and put them up all over my bedroom walls.

I also had a big crush for a while on Scott Baio, the guy who played Chachi, the junior Fonzie on *Happy Days*. It was weird when I eventually came out to Hollywood and actually met Scott Baio. He turned out to be a bigger geek than Mister Rogers.

Right after encountering Scott Baio, I did a radio interview where I said I'd just met him. "Did you know," I said, "that he has a thing for Playmates?"

Well, the deejays go nuts, and start singing "Chachi loves Playmates, Chachi loves Playmates!"

The weirdest thing was that the very next night I was out to dinner with one of my girlfriends and Scott Baio appeared before me again. He walked up to our table, and I offered a "Hi, Scott."

"You f_____g bitch!" he said. "Who do you think you are?" He continued venting, and I just sank lower and lower into my chair. The next day, naturally, I called back the radio station and they did a few more choruses of "Chachi loves Playmates." I've since run into him again, but now he pretends that he doesn't even know me. But that's okay—because I can still hear that refrain—"Chachi loves Playmates, na-na-na-na!"

"Chachi loves Playmates, Chachi loves Playmates!"

A lot of times my childhood crushes revolved around rescue fantasies involving tall, dark, handsome, and heroic men. I especially loved the television show *CHiPS*, because I always thought that Ponch (Erik Estrada) was just the kind of hunky, dark-haired hero-

man for me. I loved how no matter what trouble there was in Ponch's personal life, he always found the time to save lives and help people. I once actually had a dream back then that Erik Estrada, as Ponch, saved me from some terrible tragedy and then carried me off into the sunset. What the hell was I thinking?

Right around age twelve, though, things started getting weird. Gee, I wonder why that might be?

GOOD CATHOLIC

It's still really hard for me to say no to people, no matter how many times I've already said yes. It's probably my strict religious upbringing; a friend of mine calls it part of the "Mother Teresa complex" that becomes part of the way you grow up as a Catholic woman.

I was recently in Las Vegas on vacation, and in about an hour I gave out about four hundred autographs straight. When the four hundred and first person asked for a signature, I finally said no, and the guy shot back to me, "You really are a bitch!"

I was so upset! One of my biggest fears has always been that people won't like me. A good Catholic girl doesn't want to hurt anybody's feelings, no matter what the cost.

I was truly devout growing up; I wouldn't go to bed unless I said sixty Our Fathers, sixty Hail Marys, and sixty Angel of Gods. I would even pray for all the dogs in the neighborhood. Of course, I've developed a new mentality toward Catholicism since high school, where I learned that one of the points of life was to torment yourself with guilt and carry the cross until you feel like you've been forgiven.

Now I believe in looking at life as a lesson and then moving on. Why carry the weight of the world? It's too heavy. That said, there are people out there abandoning their children, not fulfilling their commitments, and generally behaving shamefully. Shouldn't they feel guilty?

I guess, but I still believe in the justice of karma, because destiny is going to come back to haunt them. I've already seen it happen. All those girls who were mean to me in high school are now making shakes at McDonald's. Screw the guilt—karma will take care of it!

Still, I'm grateful that I grew up with a belief system that gave me a good conscience and a belief in trying to do the right thing. I think that all the religion I got drilled into me as a child gave me a little head start on the rest of my generation, who grew up with no spiritual beliefs. I was forced to stay on the smooth, narrow road in Catholic school, while some people my age who grew up in a more permissive setting are taking some bumpy streets.

So many in my generation have no set of values or any notion of faith. I got that from church, but even more from my family. It gave me a grounding, a foundation that I still rely on as I go through valueless Hollywood. Maybe that's why I still have such mixed emotions about my whole *Playboy* experience, getting breast implants and playing the games you have to play to get ahead here. While I don't feel as guilty as I used to about not going to church as regularly as I did in Chicago, I still have a little question in the back of my head about whether I'm going to burn in hell for my various sins.

My own Mother Teresa is my mother. She taught me about love, and she is the reason that I am so touchy feely, lovey-dovey with everyone in my life. I'll feel her presence even when I'm onstage, and I'll want to start crying.

To this day, the worst single thing that's happened to me is when I temporarily broke her heart by posing for *Playboy*. I wrote my parents two letters because I was at a *Playboy* convention in San Francisco when the issue came out. My sister said that my mother fell to the ground when she read the letters that I'd written to her about what I'd done. Mom literally had a nervous breakdown.

When I heard what had happened, I broke down in tears. I tried to call my mom for three days and she wouldn't speak to me. The worst part was that my sister said that my mom cried out at one point, "At least I have three more daughters."

That hurt so bad—my mommy!

I thought my life was over. I thought that I had never screwed up so badly as when I walked into the *Playboy* building. Still, I didn't give up hope, and she finally called me back five days later, after two out of her eighty million friends said it was okay that I'd posed.

"I think it was horrible what you did," she said, "but you're my daughter and I'm going to stick by you." But to have your best friend in the world disown you, even temporarily, was the most horrible moment of my life.

JUSTICE, SOUTH SIDE OF CHICAGO-STYLE

Suddenly, you're in the seventh grade and **everything** starts happening. It's just terrible. But because you're in this strict Catholic family, of course you don't talk about IT. Sex. Your body. Women and men.

Please pass the potatoes, Mom.

Because I had no information about anything except the proper way to chant your catechism, I had no idea what was happening when I first got my period. I quite literally thought I was going to die, because it felt like someone was shredding my intestines with razor blades. The pain was horrible, and I just cried and cried for seven hours until I finally realized what was going on. Little Jenny is a woman!

Anyway, I started getting boobs, which immediately freaked me out. I just woke up one morning and there they were—two little bumps that looked like zits. I didn't know what to do. I just stood in front of the mirror and tried to push them back into my chest, hoping and praying they'd just go away.

In the coming months I would try to do anything to make them disappear. I would wear three T-shirts to school to try to hide them; it didn't matter that I was dripping with sweat. I didn't want any of the boys to know what was happening to me!

When I think back to that time, all I remember is this overwhelming sense of humiliation about my breasts. And then you're in high school, and of course you're praying for them.

I started getting boobs, which immediately freaked me out.

I just woke up one morning and there they were—two little bumps that looked like zits.

Mom, me, and Joanne

THE FIRST BOY I EVER KISSED WAS GARY MANZO, WHO MADE HIS BIG MOVE AFTER SCHOOL ONE DAY WHEN WE WERE BOTH IN SEVENTH GRADE.

I didn't really have any enemies back then, except for the girls with big boobs. God, how I envied them. Mary DeRushka had big boobs in grammar school, and all the boys loved her for it. Nobody ever paid any attention to me, so of course I was really jealous.

I just had a really hard time getting boys to like me when I was young, which made me feel even more not cool. It's all so stupid now, but, God, the pain my unpopularity with the guys caused me back then.

How did I ever get over the torment that groovy-guy Barry Belinsky, who I'd had a terrible schoolgirl crush on, didn't like me back in grammar school?

I don't know. But I did. And then, a few months ago, I went back to my grammar school reunion and there was Barry Belinsky himself, fat and ugly and missing a few teeth. Well, of course he came up and said hi, and I just told him, "Yeah, right, buddy—I bet you feel like a jackass now!"

I was in my karmic glory. But it took me this long to realize that I'm glad those cool guys never liked me, because in fact they were rather creepy.

Still, I guess I wasn't a total loser back then. The first boy I ever kissed was Gary Manzo, who made his big move after school one day when we were both in seventh grade. We were in the alley behind my best friend Sarah's house, and he kind of nonchalantly asked me if I'd ever kissed anybody before.

"Oh, sure," I said. Little did he know that I was as pure as my white church dress. And I certainly didn't tell him that only an hour before I'd actually been practicing my first kiss by sticking my tongue into my own balled-up fist and slurping around for the pay dirt that I was certain lay somewhere deep inside the forbidden territory of making out with a neighborhood boy.

Anyway, we did it—we made out for a few minutes behind Sarah's garage. I then immediately ran home and brushed my teeth for half an hour. I was so disgusted that I quite literally almost threw up.

Still, even in junior high school it seemed like the girls with the big boobs always got the best guys. I hated them for that, especially Renee Clemenza, who not only had

WE MADE OUT FOR A FEW MINUTES BEHIND SARAH'S GARAGE. I THEN IMMEDIATELY RAN HOME AND BRUSHED MY TEETH FOR HALF AN HOUR. I WAS SO DISGUSTED THAT I QUITE LITERALLY ALMOST THREW UP.

big boobs but whom I also once caught making out with my boyfriend, Bob, at the Ford City mall.

Of course, I had to drag Renee out of there by her hair and beat the living bejeesus out of her. Justice, South Side of Chicago–style.

That happened when I was fifteen and was walking through the Ford City mall, my home base off my block and the center of the universe as I moved from kid to teenager. I was taking an unannounced stroll by myself after school one day through its corridors when I saw Renee Clemenza deep in the rapture of kissing my boyfriend over by the mall's telephone banks.

"Holy crap, there's Jenny!!" I remember Renee yelling.

At first I froze, all intimidated, and then I started sweating. And suddenly my Irish temper started whirring and raging, and I got pissed off like I'd never been before in my life. The world started moving in slow motion, and I calmly walked up to them and confronted Renee.

Sad but true—you always go for the person that's cheating with your partner. Reacting thusly, I grabbed a hunk of Renee's hair and dragged her outside the mall and started wailing on her. It was quite a butt-stomping: I still remember mall security running outside like a SWAT team and finally pulling me off her.

"I'm sorry, Jenny—he came after me; I didn't want to," Renee cried as I bared my fangs one last time at her.

"Okay," I said, having refound my spiritual calm, "I'm sorry too. I got a little bit out of control. I just don't want to ever see you near him again."

The mall was our village and second home, and having caught Renee kissing my boyfriend there was the same as catching them making out on the couch in my parents' basement. I was a mall rat, and to disrespect me there was the same as doing it in my own home.

The arcade at the Ford City mall was the place where all the boys and girls would fix each other up. Eventually, I forgave Bob his infidelity, and, once again, many nights we could be found dining downstairs at the mall's food court.

Our romance continued smoothly, and a couple of weeks later we were having dinner together at the mall. Suddenly, the head head-banger of this Chicago gang called the Popes walked over to our table and said to my boyfriend, "I want to go out with your girlfriend."

Now, my boyfriend, I must say, was not a steroid monster. I actually think that's why I liked him—because he was so quiet and mousy. Still, he did try to assert his manliness when confronted by the baddest gang-banger any of us had ever seen.

"Uh, no," my boyfriend said.

The gang guy nodded, then picked up my boyfriend by his neck and dragged him. Then he started bashing Bob's head against a brick wall in the parking lot. His nose was broken immediately, and suddenly there was this geyser of blood spurting out everywhere.

MY BOYFRIEND, I MUST SAY, WAS NOT A STEROID MONSTER. I ACTUALLY THINK THAT THAT'S WHY I LIKED HIM—BECAUSE HE WAS SO QUIET AND MOUSY.

Seeing four bones sticking out of my boyfriend's nose, I reacted as any proud Chicago girl would. I jumped on the gang-banger's back and started hitting and kicking him. Well, out came the mall police, who separated everybody. The king of the Popes took off, but my boyfriend spent the rest of the day in the hospital.

And then, a month later, I dumped him. Sorry!

the
mccarthy

lynette

dad

jenny

joanne

mom

amy

family

MY TROPHY MOM

I guess that one of the keys to understanding my own childhood is that I come from a family that includes six uncles who were priests and four aunts who were nuns. This doesn't mean that they were by definition jerks: some of the best people I've met in my life have been priests and nuns.

My favorite priest wasn't a relation, but he did work in our parish and he eventually came to feel like family. Father Marky was his name, and he was the kind of hip priest who hung out at night with the kids at the mall arcade and was just really cool in every way. One of my goofiest memories of Father Marky is running into him right after I first appeared in *Playboy*.

Oh, my God, do I need to go to confession? I recall thinking in my panic as I said hello to him. The funny thing is that he actually asked me for an autographed copy of *Playboy*. I still remember what I wrote on the cover:

"Dear Father Marky," I began. "Forgive me, Father, for I have sinned. Love, Jenny McCarthy." I've since heard from reliable sources that that autograph is still hanging in a prized spot in the parish rectory.

The clergy in my own family were much stricter; one of my uncles actually wrote me a letter after I posed nude in *Playboy* telling me that I'd been excommunicated from the family. Thank God my parents and siblings aren't so judgmental and self-righteous.

Without a doubt, my most treasured possession on this earth is my mother. I really don't know what I'm going to do when she dies, which, God willing, won't be for another 150 years. I have no idea how I'll get by on this earth without her.

I know I'm gushing, but she really is everything to me. In my mind, my mom is just like Mrs. June Cleaver and Wonder Woman and all of my favorite superheroes combined into one person. Early on she decided to stay home to raise her four little girls, a job that she did wonderfully.

Thank God she wasn't ever one of those materialistic moms, or our family would have never survived. I swear, she didn't buy herself any new clothes for twenty years just so all her kids could have cool Reeboks. I'd go to school and all my friends' moms would be wearing Chanel clothes and expensive perfume, and my mom would be wearing Kmart jeans and Secret deodorant as her cologne.

WITHOUT A DOUBT,
MY MOST TREASURED POSSESSION
ON THIS EARTH IS MY MOTHER.

To this day, I just want to put her in a trophy case on my shelf and stare at her all day long. She's so totally full of love, and someday I want to be just like her.

Mom never once shot down with words or actions my dreams of one day being a famous movie star. This, despite the obvious fact that I wasn't even the star of her own four daughters.

I can't help but laugh when I remember that every Halloween she'd indulge my tacky wonts and help me dress up as a movie star. So, every single year I'd wear this same long blond wig and long red gown and go parading around the neighboring blocks with my cigar and goodie bag, a seven-year-old who, when asked what she was dressed up as, would say, "I'm a movie star named Jenny."

My dad, meanwhile, is a typical Irishman. He's short and cute and looks sort of like Mr. Magoo. He loves to golf, fish, and drink at the pub with his buddies, who all call him Macky.

My childhood memory of him that I always carry with me is him walking in the door from work and shouting, "Where are my hugs?" All four of his girls would jump up and grab an arm or a leg and just squeeze. He is a great dad, and he always gave each of his girls so much love.

I was really close to him growing up, but he was always the quiet one in the family. My mom was the one who yelled at the kids and punished us, the one who would play both family cop and psychologist, the one who demanded replies to her questions of "What's going on in your life?" or "What in God's name is wrong with you today, Jenny?"

(Top Left) Here I am with Mom and Amy, celebrating Amy's kindergarten graduation *(Top Right)* Mom and me going for a ride

JENNY

BIRTH Jenny
McCarthy

:)

GOD BLESS

Baby: McCarthy
Born: 11/1/72 at: 12:42 pm
Weight: 6 lbs. 6 oz.
Length: 19

The Nurseries
of the
Little Company of Mary Hospital
Evergreen Park 42, Illinois

MY DAD, MEANWHILE, IS A TYPICAL IRISHMAN.... MY CHILDHOOD MEMORY OF HIM THAT I ALWAYS CARRY WITH ME IS HIM WALKING IN THE DOOR FROM WORK AND SHOUTING...

Dad with his four daughters: back: Lynette, middle: me, right: JoJo, bottom: Amy

My dad's style was much more along the lines of Al Bundy in *Married . . . with Children*. He was sort of a couch potato who liked to sack out in front of the television with one hand stuck down his pants, speaking only to say things like, "Honey, could you pass me the remote control?"

Being strict Catholics, my parents naturally never breathed a word to us about sex. I can still recall the stricken look on my mother's face the day I came home from kindergarten and told her, "I know what sex is, Mom."

My mother looked like she was going to pass out. "What did you learn?" she demanded.

"Sex," I said, "is when the guy puts his thingy in the girl's thingy." I had no idea what that meant; for all I knew it could have meant the guy put his finger in the girl's ear.

My mother, however, was horrified. She couldn't believe that the family was spending almost every cent they had on private Catholic school educations and her daughter was coming home from kindergarten with sex talk on her lips. From that point on, she never once breathed a single word about the birds and the bees to any of her daughters. I had to learn everything the good old-fashioned American way—in the streets—where the rest of my world lived.

"WHERE ARE MY HUGS?"

LEFTOVER FOOD UNDER THE BED AND LYNETTE'S UNDERWEAR

To be honest, I think my dad could have gone batty living in a small house surrounded by five very animated women. Still, the lack of males in our home never really struck me as weird. The only time I really wished I had a brother was in high school, when girls would follow me home from school just so they could beat me up. It would have been nice to have a brother to defend me, but instead I learned how to put up my dukes and take care of myself. That's not a bad thing to know how to do.

We only had one bathroom, if you can imagine that, in our house. So picture, if you can, what a living hell it was in the morning when everybody was trying to get up and out of the house.

It was pandemonium every single day as we all fought to get into that one little bathroom, which even when it was empty overflowed with five different kinds of curling irons, hair sprays, and deodorants. Mornings in our bathroom looked like a *Three Stooges* episode, with doors flying open and shut and things flying all over the place.

Still, everybody knew McCarthy House Commandment Number One. No matter how far any of the girls were into their morning showers, you got out of that bathroom the second Dad was awake and ready to get ready for work at the steel plant.

Since the day I was born, I guess, I was pretty much the slob of the family. I used to share a room with my older sister, Lynette, and it used to drive her insane when I'd just throw my dirty clothes and socks into a pile that literally grew to the ceiling. I was always as lazy as Lynette was meticulous (and sensitive!), and over the years I did whatever I could to drive her completely crazy.

I always used to leave food all over the room, and instead of taking my dishes back down to the kitchen when I was done eating, I'd just hide the leftover food

> ## McCarthy House Commandment Number One:
>
> **NO MATTER HOW FAR ANY OF THE GIRLS WERE INTO THEIR MORNING SHOWERS, YOU GOT OUT OF THAT BATHROOM THE SECOND DAD WAS AWAKE.**

My favorite Picture

my favorite shirt

with Amy

Lynette

Jo-Jo

Mom

Lynette

Lynette Amy

me

Lynette

me

Joanne

Our 1st pool at Amy home

Lynette

Joanne Joanne

Amy

me

under my bed. It would start to smell, and by the time Lynette would discover it, there would be penicillin growing on it. That was when we'd get into some pretty huge fights. Sorry about that, Lynette.

My parents tried to cure me of my slobbiness by embarrassing the living crap out of me. One year in high school my entire extended family came over to our house for Christmas. It was then that my mother thought it would be a good idea to give everyone a guided tour of the mess I kept in my room.

So, while I looked on in horror, all my relatives trooped upstairs, went into my room, and started pulling dirty sheets, underwear, and plates of old food from under my bed and from atop piles of trash. That was the single most embarrassing thing my parents ever did to me. But what a great wake-up call.

Poor Lynette, my sister who shared a bedroom with me during my piggiest years. We fought early and often over the cleanliness issue. Our biggest battle occurred one morning when I borrowed a pair of Lynette's underwear and wore them to Mother McAuley, the Catholic school we both went to.

> MY PARENTS TRIED TO CURE ME OF MY SLOBBINESS BY **EMBARRASSING** THE LIVING CRAP OUT OF ME.

Every morning—no lie—Lynette would count the underwear in her drawer, and that day she came up one pair short. I'd already taken off for school, so she tracked me down like a bounty hunter in one of the school's hallways and started yelling.

She tackled me to the floor, wrestled me to a pin, and then started ripping the underwear right off my body. So, there I was, lying in the hallway with my skirt up, spread-eagled, while all the girls in the school walked by and said, "Wow, look at Jenny—I guess she shouldn't wear her sister's underwear!"

GRANDPA: BUTT GRABBER

Well, of course I was thrilled when *USA Today* (March 18, 1997) ran a huge feature on my two basketball-playing, superstar little sisters, Joanne and Amy. Jo-Jo just graduated this spring from the University of Illinois at Chicago, where she broke the all-time school scoring record. She's going to keep at it; right now she's playing professionally in Europe. Go, Jo!

The Sisters McCarthy

What's it like to be Jenny McCarthy's sisters? Amy and Joanne leave TV stardom to their famous sister. They've found their niche on the basketball court. Page 2D.

By Anne Ryan, USA TODAY

In Chicago: Amy, left, and Joanne play ball for the University of Illinois.

Amy just finished her sophomore year at the University of Illinois at Chicago, and she's as good a ballplayer (and just as cute) as Joanne. I'm so glad that both my sisters were honest in the *USA Today* article about what it's like to be related to me.

"At away games," the reporter wrote, "[people] in the stands will shout things like 'We want Jenny! We love Jenny.' Do they get sick of that?"

"Sometimes," Joanne said.

And then Amy had to give me the business in print. "Growing up we'd play church and Jenny would be the priest," she said. "She was funny as a priest."

I think the person I was most similar to in my entire family was my late grandfather. He was really quite nuts and crazy, and I'm quite sure I got a lot of the parts of my personality that you see on television from him. Grandpa was an old-style Polish hunk: he was six foot five, a tall, tan, muscular old man who had tattoos of naked women all down his arm.

I remember that all he would ever do, no matter where we went when I was little, was flirt with any and all visible women. We'd go to the grocery store, and all of a sudden I'd look up and see this sixty-five-year-old man chasing old women down the aisles, trying to pinch their butts. He'd get down on one knee and launch into song in front of the cashiers. He would fall in love in a second, and he seemed to derive special pleasure from cooking up the most outlandish things he could think of in order to embarrass me publicly.

One day in grammar school I even brought Grandpa in for "show and tell" because I truly thought he was the most amazing thing I'd ever seen. He, of course, ate up the attention of a fresh and captive audience.

As soon as he got up to the front of the room he started singing "Popeye the Sailor Man." He then started dancing a jig and reached out to grab my teacher's butt. Everybody in the class was actually pretty freaked out, because they were used to grandfathers with twinkly eyes who were all wise and calm and tired.

And here was my beloved, ancient grandpa, dancing around the room, yelling at my kindergarten teacher, "Yeah, baby, whoooo! Look at those buns!"

He was wild, I've heard, all his life. When my mother was in kindergarten, she once told me, she was assigned to draw a scene from the Bible. My grandfather volunteered to do her homework himself; when my mom took the picture to class, her teacher began hyperventilating.

What good old Granddad Butt Grabber had drawn was a scene of Adam and Eve in the garden. So far, so good. But instead of having Adam taking a bite of the apple, he had portrayed the first man taking a leak onto that sacred tree. Oops!

To some, his routine may not sound so different from my role as co-host on *Singled Out*. Maybe, maybe not. But I certainly did get a lot of what I bring to the screen from him, which is only one of the reasons I still miss my old grandpa a lot, every day.

Grandpa Jenny

Graham

I think the person I was most similar to in my entire family was my late grandfather.

DAD AND DENNY'S: MY FAVORITE FISHING TRIP

My dad, on the other hand, was definitely not into making scenes. Above all else he liked peace and quiet, and his favorite outings with the girls usually involved little fishing trips where we could all listen to the silence of the lake.

It felt like a big adventure when I was little; we'd all wake up at about four in the morning, load up the car, and then drive about an hour outside of Chicago to go bass and walleye fishing. It was really fun, and usually really calming, just sitting in the fishing boat with my dad, my sisters, and a can of worms.

One fishing trip, however, was anything but mellow. We were all on the way to the lake one morning when my dad said, "Hey, why don't we stop at this Denny's restaurant and get some breakfast? Wouldn't that be good?"

Lynette, who was eight, and I, who was six, agreed that nothing had ever sounded better. So we went into the Denny's at five in the morning, took a booth, ordered our food, and waited.

Suddenly, this heavily sweating, freaky-looking guy staggered into the restaurant and plopped down in the booth directly across from us. I could tell a scene was developing, and I noticed that my dad was getting a little uncomfortable.

Then some wise guy sitting at the table on the other side of the freak leaned over and asked this weirdo, "Are you okay, buddy?"

The wise guy was sitting at a table with a bunch of sniggering buddies, and was apparently giving the sweating freak a razzing just to impress his friends. The freak, however, was not amused.

He got up, went over to the guy, and BOOM—knocked him out with one blow. Blood was spurting everywhere. So then one of the guy's buddies got up to challenge the freak. BOOM—the pal went down, unconscious too.

Next in line was the Denny's cook, a big, gnarly guy who came running out of the kitchen yelling, "What's going on out here?" BOOM—the cook was knocked out, too.

Now, imagine this scene: my sister and me, two little girls, being shielded from the trouble by my father. But then, all of a sudden, Lynette went a little mental. Lynette can get freaked out by a mosquito, so it wasn't really that much of a surprise when she stood up in the middle of all this and started screaming at the top of her lungs.

She then jumped out of her chair, vaulted over the three bleeding and unconscious bodies on the floor, ran into the parking lot, and jumped on top of our car. My dad was kind of freaking out— should he chase after Lynette in the parking lot, or should he stay with me? By then I was under the table holding my little butter knife like a machete.

Finally, a bunch of men, including my father, bum-rushed the freak and dragged him outside. The police finally came and handcuffed him, but it wasn't until he was safely away in the patrol car that I finally put down my butter knife and began to breathe like a normal human being again.

My dad then shrugged and simply herded Lynette back into Denny's. Then we all just sat there silently eating our breakfasts like nothing had happened. I can't remember whether we caught any fish that day, but this bizarre tale of love and fists inside a Denny's at dawn remains my all-time favorite fishing story.

MY DAD'S FAVORITE OUTINGS
WITH THE GIRLS USUALLY
INVOLVED LITTLE FISHING TRIPS
WHERE WE COULD ALL LISTEN
TO THE SILENCE OF THE LAKE

(Left) My first fish caught in Pennsylvania *(Right)* Me, age 11, fishing at the Minus 300 Club

HEY, DAD, HOW'S IT GOING?

It's so funny and interesting to watch how my parents have reacted to my fame. In most ways they haven't changed at all, which is both reassuring and, at times, a little frightening. I mean, I still can't believe what my mother told me one night when I called home to check in.

"Hi, Mom, what's going on?" I asked her when she picked up the phone.

"Oh, well," she said, "some people from that television show *American Journal* came over today."

"What? Ma, are you kidding?" I said, horrified. "You didn't let them in the house, did you?"

"Yeah, I invited them in," my mother said. "They wanted to talk to us, so I let them in, sat them down, and made them some coffee."

"Oh, no, Mom!" I said. "Don't you know that *American Journal* is one of those tabloid television shows?"

"I know, Jenny," my mother said, "but they seemed so polite. They stayed for three and a half hours. They wouldn't leave, so we just kept talking."

"MOM!!" I said. "What did you talk about?"

"Well," she said, "we talked a lot about you. I told them about how dirty you kept your room in high school and I took them upstairs to see it. I also showed them some pictures in the scrapbook."

Yep, that's my mother. And that's how *American Journal* got its inside scoop on the private life of Jenny McCarthy.

Then my father got on the line, and we had a very typical conversation.

"Hey, Dad," I said. "How's it going?"

"Fine."

"How's work?"

"Sucks."

"What are you doing this weekend?"

"Like to go golf."

"How's your golf game, Dad?"

"Good."

"How're the kid sisters?"

"Fine."

"Cool, Dad, great," I said. "Can I talk to Ma again?"

For better or worse, that's my dad. Not a great conversationalist. I used to marvel at the ways my parents communicated or, more accurately, didn't communicate. It was never really a bad thing—it just seemed a little strange that they never talked about anything except how to get through the next day with a roof still over our family's head.

I knew they loved each other, but I never had the feeling that they shared their inner lives with each other. Still, I learned a lot from watching my parents not talk to each other. The knowledge they gave me about the importance of communication with your mate was a wonderful thing to give a child—even if what I learned is that for me to be happy I have to do things differently.

MONEY

There are obviously many great things about getting famous and making a little money. For me, the single greatest thing was paying off the bills of everyone in my family. Money was such a huge issue growing up that when I was little I would always fantasize about one day being able to write check after check to pay off my entire family's ever-increasing debts.

We were always, always, always broke—money, and the lack of it, was always the main topic of interest and horror in my house growing up. I can't remember how many times I had the following conversation with my mother when I was little:

Me: Mom, please, please, **PLEEZE**, can I have this toy?

Mom (after first digging into the bottom of her purse for change and coming up empty): No, Jenny. We don't have enough money for food, let alone that expensive toy.

Rats. So, growing up, I watched as my dad worked three jobs in order to afford private Catholic school for all the girls, and it just broke my heart to see him busting his butt like that for us. Someday, I told myself, when I'm rich and famous, I'm just going to pay off all those bills my folks never seemed able to make.

And then, at the end of 1996, I was actually able to do it. That felt so great that for weeks I actually thought I was living in a dream. That is my favorite memory of what fame has allowed me to do.

Running a close second was the time I was able to take my entire family out for a big splurge, a five-star dinner of the kind we never once had growing up. We went the whole nine yards—expensive champagne, entrées whose prices would have covered a semester at Mother McAuley, and desserts that each cost what my mother would spend to feed our entire family of six for a week.

I guess that my parents do treat me a little differently because I'm famous. I don't think it's just because I'm a "celebrity" but also because they now know how much trouble and terror I've had while making it to the top. They know the hell I went through when I was first in *Playboy*, back when it seemed that all of my relatives (and most of Chicago) hated me and were calling me a fallen sinner.

My folks went through that crap storm with me and saw me survive. Now they even call me for advice, which really makes me feel good, because I'm sure there was a time when they thought I'd probably end up behind bars or something.

I'M A VIRGIN

Still, there's one area where I continue to lie to my parents, just like in the old days. In their minds, I don't have sex. They really don't know that I do. Since I'm not married, they really think I'm a virgin. Like I said, it's the only big lie I tell them.

Of course, it helps that like all good Catholic parents they are capable of comfortably living with immense amounts of denial. To make it even easier for me, they can have very selective memories about the various misdeeds I've perpetrated over the years.

Oh, God, I still blush when I think of an interview my parents saw on CNN in 1994, when I was *Playboy*'s Playmate of the Year. It was some ridiculous relationship show, and the host kept asking me deep, probing, completely obnoxious questions about my sex life.

He then brought up the topic of orgasms, and for some reason I just went off. Suddenly, I was talking like I was Dr. Ruth Westheimer. Only, I was talking about me! I gave away every secret about my sex life, including the little factlet that I take great pride in being multiorgasmic.

IT HELPS THAT LIKE ALL GOOD CATHOLIC PARENTS THEY ARE CAPABLE OF COMFORTABLY LIVING WITH IMMENSE AMOUNTS OF DENIAL.

I knew my parents were watching me tell the world about my orgasms, and, to this day, I have no idea why I went off and was way too open. I could barely even talk to them after the show. What was I going to say—"I was just kidding"??

So I didn't say anything but, "I'm sorry, I'm really sorry, Mom and Dad."

And, as usual, they let me off the hook. All my mother ever said about the incident was, "Jenny, what are we ever going to do with you?"

The funny thing is that with their selective memories they've truly suppressed all remembrances of that memorable night. Now, I swear to God, they're back to thinking I'm still a virgin.

"Me, a virgin?" I tell my mom. "Of course! Just like you and the nuns at Mother McAuley always told me to be!"

HOLLYWOOD:

HIGH $CHOOL
with money

It's never been an industry secret that show business is exactly like high school, except with money. I say this mantra so often to myself because it reminds me that all the games people play in Hollywood are really just variants of what every desperate person in high school (me included) did to someone else back in the days of homerooms and senior proms.

I guess the basic fact to know about my high school experience is that I went to an all-girl Catholic school. Mother McAuley was renowned all over Chicago for its strict nuns and for the fact that 99 percent of its graduates also made it all the way through college (I, of course, was in that lost 1 percent). One other thing Mother McAuley was famous for was a student body that consisted of girls who were seventy pounds overweight with brown hair, retainers, and zits.

ONE OTHER THING MOTHER McAULEY WAS FAMOUS FOR WAS A STUDENT BODY THAT CONSISTED OF GIRLS WHO WERE SEVENTY POUNDS OVERWEIGHT WITH BROWN HAIR, RETAINERS, AND ZITS.

Now, I wasn't exactly Princess Grace of Monaco myself, but because I was only twenty pounds overweight and had bleached blond hair, most of the girls hated me. They all wanted to literally crucify me right in the middle of the school.

Still, I was desperate to fit in with the other girls. I think that's why I started making fun of myself for anybody who'd listen, to show everybody in high school that I was just like everybody else. By mocking myself before anybody else could get in their licks, I could show everybody in school that I didn't take myself seriously at all.

I took this attitude with me when I went to Hollywood, and I think my being able to make fun of myself is the big reason girls and young women like me even though I'm a former *Playboy* Playmate of the Year. By making fun of myself on national television, I am telling every young girl out there that you don't have to be perfect to be liked by the boys.

And one other thing. As much as I poke fun at my Catholic school days, I'm grateful because the nuns taught us to stand on our own, to be strong and independent, and to care about others. It was there that I learned to strive to become whatever I wanted to be in the world (although being a Playmate, I'm sure, was *not* what the nuns had in mind).

In the meantime, *laugh* at how ridiculous it is to be a young girl growing up in this society! It was my survival tactic in high school, and now that I'm out in Hollywood I'm really grateful for the hell I went through back in the days when I was sure I'd die miserable, friendless, and all alone because I didn't fit in with everybody else.

MAXIPADS

God, I can't believe I can now tell all these horrible high school stories and actually **laugh** at what those girls at Mother McAuley did to me. Although it's difficult for me to pick out the single most horrible moment for me in high school, probably the worst incident was the time a bunch of girls took my purse and stole a bunch of Maxipads that I had stashed in there.

"LOOK, THERE'S JENNY McCARTHY'S MAXIPAD UP NEAR THE CEILING!"

Me, age 16

These girls then took my pads and wrote "Jenny McCarthy" in large lipstick letters on all of them. From there, they took the pads and stuck them up all over the school, way up high in the hallways, so nobody could just jump up there and take them down.

So, for the whole day in school, I had to watch and listen as everybody in the building walked through the hallways and said, "Look, there's Jenny McCarthy's Maxipad up near the ceiling!"

All the kids, of course, made fun of me all day, and I can't begin to tell you how embarrassing and humiliating and actually kind of scary the whole incident really was. Finally, the nuns had to go fetch the janitor, who brought a ladder and a hook to get all of the pads down. Boy, was that a great day for my self-esteem.

ME: GIRL MOST LIKELY TO BE ADDICTED TO HAIRSPRAY, OR TWO THOUSAND GOD-FEARING VIRGINS

I'm not sure why, but sin is on my mind these days. To be honest, sin has been on my mind ever since the first moment I was conscious. For sinful thought, there is nothing like an all-girl Catholic school.

What was amazing about my alma mater Mother McAuley was that there were literally two thousand God-fearing virgins percolating inside there. I mean, everybody, me included. The ironic part of this equation is that, at the same time we were all running around in our virginal, white Catholic uniforms, everybody there was utterly obsessed with all matters sexual.

The answer is so obvious now. We all wanted to know about and experiment with sex so bad precisely because it was considered so evil. In response, and still in fear for our heavenly souls, we all became students of the science, in preparation for the day when we would no longer be sent immediately to hell for having sex.

From reports I've heard, this is true at parochial schools all over the country. It's also the reason why graduates of Catholic girls' schools always know how to give really good blow jobs.

They study!

The old legend is true, I think, that Catholic schoolgirls are usually the wildest. Again, it's only logical: we were so restricted by the nuns for nine hours a day inside of our stuffy classrooms that at nighttime, it only made yin-yang sense for a whole lot of us to get a little wild and crazy.

> # ...at the same time we were all running around in our virginal, white Catholic uniforms, everybody there was utterly obsessed with all matters sexual.

During this time, the only form of evil that I regularly indulged in at school was cheating. If you took a poll of my classmates as to what they remember of me, the first thing they'd probably say is that I didn't have many friends. The second thing they'd come up with is that I cheated.

I must say that I was pretty damn good at it. Our school uniforms featured long plaid skirts, and I discovered early on that I could write every answer to every test on my leg and hide the evidence under my lengthy skirt. I was also quite good during a test at looking as if I were innocently staring down at my answer sheet, trying to figure out the right response.

In fact, I would be reading off a little cheat sheet on my lap. I got very good at writing very small on infinitesimal-sized pieces of paper, just like those monks who try to inscribe the Bible on the head of a pin. I never really got busted badly by a teacher for cheating, but my talent was well known.

Indeed, my bad habit was probably the only notoriety I ever got from anybody in high school. Why? Because in my desire to find popularity, I would freely give cheat sheets to any and all girls who wanted them.

It was as if I was screaming, "Like me, *please*!!"

But they didn't. I don't remember what I was voted "most likely" to be in my high school yearbook — probably "girl most likely to get addicted to hairspray." I can't help laughing whenever I look at any picture ever taken of me in high school, because I always had huge, monstrous hair.

Every morning I would have to spray on about half a can of Aquanet extra, extra, extra hold—that hair stuff that smells like bug spray mixed with Agent Orange. My hair was typically so stiff that boys in the neighborhood used to try to set it on fire by flicking lit matches at my head from ten feet away.

"GIRL MOST LIKELY TO GET ADDICTED TO HAIRSPRAY."

They never succeeded, though some of the girls at Mother McAuley did spit gum and hawk loogies into my hair. But nobody, any where, any time, ever brought the big thing completely down. Let me tell you, girls, life ain't always easy when you're a dedicated big-haired woman.

Tragedy, however, struck my hair during my last two years in high school. As it happened, my mom's a hairdresser who got her beauty license, then immediately had four babies. Instead of leaving us during the day so that she could work at a beauty parlor, Mom opened a little salon for the neighborhood ladies in the kitchen of our little house.

Being a professional, Mom took great pride in doing up all the girls' hair every morning before school. This all worked out just fine until I got to the eleventh grade and suddenly perms were the big and most necessary thing for any self-respecting Mother McAuley student to wear.

Well, my hair was really straight, but I begged Mom to give me a perm. My hair was already bleached, but she came up with her own secret formula for applying the perm solution so that all the different chemicals would get along. Unfortunately, she left the perm solution in my hair for an hour when she should have washed it out after five minutes. I *hate* when that happens!

Imagine my surprise when I looked in the mirror that morning to discover that I was now the proud owner of a blond Afro. The top of my head was such an unmitigated nightmare that for the last two years of high school I had to wear my hair in a French braid.

Senior prom, naturally, was another horror show. I'd gone on spring break to Florida earlier that year and met some guy who got drunk with a bunch of girlfriends and me at a bar one night. He was going back

My high school prom date, Bob, from Long Island

home to New York the next morning, but for some reason I gave him my phone number. (Okay, I know the reason. I gave him my number because I was drunk. Girls, take note.)

Anyway, the guy actually dared to call me at home the next week.

"Hey," he said, "why don't I come to Chicago for your senior prom? I can be your date."

Well, my boyfriend at the time took *his* Spring Break Slut Affair to *his* prom, so I figured what's good for the goose is good for the gander. So, like an idiot, I told the guy from New York that I'd go with him. It was pretty nuts, because I really didn't know this guy from Adam, and I'd been totally drunk when I gave him my phone number.

Still, he flew out from New York and escorted me like a gentleman. Still, I must rank that evening as the worst night of my life. Of course, no one in my class talked to me the entire night, and nobody talked to him either (then again, nobody could understand his Long Island accent).

It didn't really matter, though, because I still missed my little high school sweetheart.

GRADUATION:
MY EMANCIPATION FROM HELL

Then again, maybe graduation day at Mother McAuley was my biggest high school nightmare. There were eight hundred of us graduating that day, and I remember that we all had to wear these long, white formal gowns, because naturally we were all virgins.

So they called off the names alphabetically, one by one, while we waited on the stage for our diplomas that would signal that this part of our lives was at last over. I was so happy to be there, because for four years I'd been praying for that day to come. That day would be my emancipation from hell, my parole date signifying that I would never have to be around these mean, cliquey girls again.

For four long years I just kept looking at the calendar, figuring out how many days were left until graduation. I focused on that day as my way of getting through the horrors, and when that day finally came I felt like a truck had been lifted off my chest.

So commencement commenced, and soon the principal was up to Molly McCarthy, the girl right in front of me. Molly was really popular, and I remember being amazed at hearing everybody screaming, "Yea, go Molly!" as soon as her name was called. And then it was my turn.

"Jennifer McCarthy."

Nothing. Silence. Not one handclap. And then, from way back in the auditorium, I hear the lone voice of my mother yelling, "Yeah, Jenny!"

That was cool, but that was my first and last graduation hurrah. I then hurried back to my chair, humiliated one last time by my own high school. Or so I thought. When I opened the little album they'd given me, I discovered that they'd purposely neglected to put a diploma inside.

Instead, there was a note from the principal informing me that if I ever wanted to get my diploma, I'd have to come in over the summer and serve all the leftover detention time I'd accumulated in my years of playing class clown.

Now I wasn't a dope; it just happened that my favorite subject in school was lunch. Can I help it if I have a delicate metabolism? I actually did pretty well with my grades: I think I made the honor roll every single semester. My only F ever was in public speaking, which of course I couldn't even begin to succeed at because of my still crippling phobia.

Despite the fact that I still sort of dreamed of one day being a star, I simply could not stand up in front of a crowd and say a word. I would literally faint. That's what happened the one time I tried public speaking. I got up, adjusted the pages of my speech, looked at the class, and began hyperventilating. I passed out, and when I woke up I learned that I'd failed the class.

Because of my fear of public speaking I couldn't even begin to think of auditioning for any of the school plays. I had always wanted to do theater, so it really made me envious when I'd see all the other girls just go to the auditions, walk up onstage, and start singing. I would sit in the back of the auditorium and just sigh and wish that I had the courage to go up there and show everybody what I could do.

So I never appeared in a single school play. Unless, that is, you count the pilgrim I played in our third-grade Thanksgiving pageant. I don't count it, personally, because the role was a nonspeaking, nonunion cameo.

Still, I could make a noise or two when I was pushed to it. The worst screaming match I ever had in high school happened at a dance where some chick walked past me, then doubled back when she thought I'd disrespected her or something. (I hadn't.) Anyway, she came right up to me and started yelling at me about how I better not look at her funny ever again or I'd meet the end of her fist.

Now this was a big girl; she was at least a foot taller then me, and must have outweighed me by seventy pounds. I knew she could kick my butt, but I was also aware that if I gave in and surrendered, I'd be bullied by this wide ride for the rest of high school. I figured my only strategy was to shout back twice as loud, to prove to porky just how tough I was (or at least pretended to be).

So I looked straight up at her and let loose with many shrill decibels of noise in which I undoubtably took the Lord's name in vain (even while sinning, I always kept track of the commandments I was breaking).

I LOOKED STRAIGHT UP AT HER AND LET LOOSE WITH MANY SHRILL DECIBELS OF NOISE IN WHICH I UNDOUBTABLY TOOK THE LORD'S NAME IN VAIN (EVEN WHILE SINNING, I ALWAYS KEPT TRACK OF THE COMMANDMENTS I WAS BREAKING).

Amazingly, my little fit worked. This girl was scared enough of my now obvious insanity that she just turned tail and walked away. Ha! Nobody ever outscreamed Jenny McCarthy!

Still, I really wasn't a bad student. I'd always respected books and learning; it was just that if I wasn't interested in a subject — or the way a teacher was presenting it — then my mind would wander to places far and unknown. And if real life intervened, I had no problem, every once in a while, with playing hooky.

I remember once when I got into a fight with my boyfriend, Tony, and I just couldn't make it through the morning at school. He'd told me the night before that he was breaking up with me, and I was so distraught the next day that I just stood at my locker bawling. When the first school bell rang, I simply moved my melodrama to the bathroom, where I stopped crying in despair and actually started barfing in grief.

I knew Tony was playing hooky from school that day himself, so after I cleaned myself up in the bathroom I called him on a pay phone and begged him to let me come over to his house and allow me to repent. No, Tony said, I don't ever want to see you again.

"Pleeeeeze??" I continued, begging. I just couldn't take it. I felt like I was going to die if Tony didn't take me back.

Finally, I took my mom's car and drove over to his house to beg for forgiveness in person for whatever I'd done. Tony at last relented, and we kissed. I felt like a real outlaw when he then called up my school and pretended he was my father. "Jenny won't be making it in today," he said. "She's not feeling well."

Tony, Tony, Tony. Through most of high school I was Tony's girl. It was the first (and last!) time in my life that I was actually wrapped around a guy's finger. Still, I had some other plans up my sleeve to become incredibly popular.

REJECTION

Early on in high school I decided that the key to my somehow fitting in would be by becoming a cheerleader. I mean, everybody loves cheerleaders, right? Not!

In Chicago, the Catholic girls' schools provided cheerleaders for the Catholic boys' schools, so I figured all I had to do to become hip was to make it past one of the cheerleading auditions that were held at the beginning of the school year.

I went to auditions at a bunch of different boys' schools for two straight years and never made the cut. It was utterly devastating to me. I'm long over the disappointment; for God's sake, I've got my own NBC sitcom now. But I can still recall, always with a painful twinge, how I thought that I was a bigger loser than even I had ever thought. My life sucked before I got cut from cheerleading, I thought, but now it was ruined.

Finally, in the months before senior year, I remember praying to God every single night to let me make the cheerleading team *somewhere*. I really pulled out all the stops—I even started praying to the soul of my dead grandmother to call upon the heavenly powers to help me out and get me on a team.

And then, as if by a miracle, I was named to be captain of the cheerleaders at Brother Rice Catholic boys' school. Of course, I never did get more popular with the girls back at my own school. Instead, they started spreading rumors that I was sleeping with the entire football team.

All of a sudden girls started coming out of the woodwork, accusing me of sleeping with their boyfriends. This was utterly untrue, but try explaining that to your mother after five crank callers in one night have told her in graphic detail what sexual acts you've supposedly been performing with whom.

Having to deal with all those ridiculous lies toughened me up, and I don't just mean mentally. After I became a cheerleader, girls would wait for me out in the parking lot after school and try to beat me up because they'd heard stories about me. Indeed, it was out on that pavement where I developed a lot of the physical skills you see on old episodes of *Singled Out* and *The Jenny McCarthy Show*.

Every day someone new would come up to me, push me, and say, "I hear you slept with my boyfriend."

"I don't *think* so," I'd say. "I wouldn't be tempted to touch your boyfriend if you paid me."

And then they'd inevitably punch me, and I'd have to defend myself. I'd put up my

I went to auditions at a bunch of different boys' schools for two straight years and never made the cut.

And then, as if by a miracle, I was named to be captain of the cheerleaders.

Of course, I never did get more popular with the girls back at my own school. Instead, they started spreading rumors that I was sleeping with the entire football team.

dukes and beat the crap out of them just like Wonder Woman. How deluded was I?

JENNY, THE LITTLE ENGINE THAT COULD NEVER STOP TRYING

Except for cheerleading, I never joined any school-related clubs, organizations, or sports teams. I was a total jock during those years and I had a blast playing softball, baseball, field hockey, and track and field with my park district teams. I even started studying martial arts.

I kind of liked that nobody at school knew what a good athlete I was, which I proved every day in the park leagues. Weirdly, I didn't even want my parents to come to any of my games. I'm not sure why, because now I would really love it if they came out here and watched me tape some of the shows that I do. But back then I couldn't stand the idea of them watching. It would have made me too nervous.

Still, despite boycotting virtually everything having to do with high school, I counted it as a great learning experience that I'd actually made the high school cheerleading squad after years of being told that I sucked at everything. I know it sounds queer, but making that team really taught me never to stop trying, even when everybody around you is telling you to quit attempting to achieve something because you don't have the talent or the looks or the right attitude to make it.

Well, I did make it, finally, and it felt so great after

103

forever being told that I wasn't good enough to be a cheerleader. I just tried and tried again, and it just goes to show you, kids, don't give up.

Now, I know this sounds grotesquely sappy, but it's true. Or let me give you another example.

Minutes before I walked uninvited into *Playboy* magazine headquarters in Chicago for the interview that would change my life, I'd had a brief meeting with a talent scout for one of Chicago's leading modeling agencies. It was at that meeting that I was told that I looked too much like a cow for any photographer anywhere to want to pay to take my picture.

I began looking at myself as Jenny, the little engine that could. Later, MTV didn't even want to look at me for a part on *Singled Out* because they thought I was just some idiot *Playboy* bunny with the IQ of a houseplant. But I insisted that my manager, Ray, persuade them to at least take a look at me . . . and look what happened.

All of it, the good with the bad, has been part of my ongoing education. If I hadn't learned how to persevere in high school, I doubt if I would have lasted until lunchtime when I finally got to Hollywood.

What goes around comes around, and you better believe the universe, in some way, is keeping score.

I know it must sound like I'm pretty bitter about the way I was treated by everybody in high school, but I really think I've moved past it and now understand that I learned some of my most valuable life lessons there. Forgive, forget, and move on, that's my motto.

Then again, what goes around comes around. I'm not into revenge, but I must say there is some satisfaction in thinking about how I'm working in Hollywood right now and those evil ones are back home in Chicago working at Burger King. Ouch!

It's karma, baby, a notion I fully believe in. What goes around comes around, and you better believe the universe, in some way, is keeping score. Still, I try to live my life focused on sweet success, not sweet revenge.

GUILT

Not that my slate is entirely clean in the high school good-karma sweepstakes. Something I did back then to another girl has actually been on my conscience for years, and I hope that confessing my sin here might be a way of somehow making karmic amends. (I haven't actually been in a confession booth for thirteen years, but as all my friends know I am in a semiconstant state of guilt over **everything**.)

Okay, this is what's been gnawing away at me for years. There was this one girl in high school, you see, who I absolutely hated for really no good reason. Her name was Barbara, and she just bugged the hell out of me. She was a phony wannabe. She wanted to be in the popular clique as bad as I did, and there was only room for one wannabe. I just couldn't stand how she always spoke in perfect, grammatical English. I always went out of my way not to be mean to people who weren't mean to me first, but with Barbara I just couldn't control myself.

So one day I told everybody in school that Barbara was a lesbian. That was a pretty bad lie to tell about someone, and I'm sure it's why I had so much bad karma of my own in that school. Poor little Barbara, who I turned into a lesbian even though she wasn't. Sorry, Barbara.

I suppose I should try to get in touch with her to apologize, but to be honest she was the one person I couldn't wait to get away from the second high school was over. Poor Barbara . . . she just bugged the crap out of me.

POOR LITTLE BARBARA, WHO I TURNED
INTO A LESBIAN EVEN THOUGH SHE
WASN'T.
Sorry, Barbara.

WHAT'S WRONG WITH ME?

But what does all this archaeology into my past really mean? Can one really ever go home? Should you even try?

Last fall I tried. My grammar school was having its reunion, and I decided to go back to see all of the people with whom I went through my first nine years of school. As I should have expected, it was totally bizarre.

I walked into this tiny room where they were holding the reunion, and everyone inside did a double-take when I walked in. I was terrified by what I was doing to people, because every time they opened their mouths, out came not words but an incomprehensible stammer.

So, I went and stood by myself in the corner and started shaking. What's *wrong* with me? I wondered, just like old times. Do I have a booger in my nose? Did I do something terrible to these people lately?

And then I realized that all these people were just as terrified of me as I was of them. Thankfully, after about an hour, all the drinks everybody was madly swilling started to kick in, and then people started approaching me a little more normally.

Suddenly, we were all just people again. "Hey, Jenny," this one guy said, after waiting an hour to work up his courage to come over to say hi to me. "Remember when I lifted up your skirt in third grade?"

Some things, for better or worse, never change.

MY (5) BIGGEST FEARS (And How I'm Trying to Get Over Them)

Hell

Holy Christ, what if the nuns back at Mother McAuley were right after all? I think I will never get over this particular fear. I like the heat, but I think the humidity would kill me.

Critics

It was quite an hellacious experience, let me assure you, when the reviews for my new MTV show appeared after the show first aired. Do you know what it feels like to pick up *People* magazine, read a paragraph, and then have to run to the bathroom and spend the whole night vomiting? It's quite charming, especially when you're due in hair and makeup in three hours and you're doubled over with cramps and the runs because you've just been called the biggest idiot in the history of mankind.

Never in the history of the written word have so many shitty reviews been written about one little television show. I knew it was coming, that it was bound to, that it was *supposed* to, for God's sake.

Virtually all the press I'd gotten in the last year I was on *Singled Out* had been a big fat wet kiss for that funky new girl on the block. Well, that kind of positive attention could last for only so long, I knew, becuse the media needs to create a backlash as much as it needs to create new stars, doncha know.

I mean, look at Julia Roberts, for God's sake. I think she's only in her late twenties, and already she's been praised to the skies by the press, then hacked to pieces, and now she's up again. Meanwhile, they're already talking of actresses only a few years younger than she is as the "new Julia Roberts." What was so wrong with the old Julia Roberts?

So I knew my own personal crap storm of crappy press was going to come over *The Jenny McCarthy Show*. And come it did. I just didn't anticipate that virtually everybody would tear it into shreds.

I read every single review of that show, read every word about how my new piece of work sucked worse than anything that mankind had ever been exposed to short of the ebola virus. I cried, then I threw up. Then I cried some more. Then I barfed some more. You get the general idea? The critics had taken total control over me.

Now this is kind of a drag, eh, seeing that we're still in the middle of shooting the show? I mean, there I am in the studio nineteen hours a day with the two hundred people that make up my crew, each of whom has just read that they are working on the worst piece of shit in television history.

But, I knew that the show was cool and that kids would like it. It was an eclectic and weird comedy show, and I was proud that I was actually able to get the sucker off the ground in the first place. MTV gave me about a month to put the whole show together, and I didn't know shit about how one went about creating out of thin air something as big as this was supposed to be.

But I went ahead and did it. I hired Joel Gallen as executive producer, and we just put together what we thought kids would find funny and different from all the other same old, same old garbage that gets churned out on TV. Slowly I came out of my deep depression. People started coming up to me and saying, "Ya know, Jen, it's cool."

MTV, thank God, was cool. It helped that the ratings were great—the best MTV ever got for a new show, they told me. They also pointed out that every new show MTV had ever put on the air had been utterly destroyed by the television critics. I mean, there would have been something wrong if those dodos *did* like the shows on MTV, doncha think? The programs are meant for fourteen-year-olds—and do you know any fourteen-year-old TV critics?

I don't *think* so.

I think I've now solved that problem by not reading my crappy reviews anymore. The state of denial, they say, is a terrible place to be, but when it comes to reading mean things strangers say about you, I say, "Lead me to denial, sweet Jesus."

I used to read all the articles about me, no matter what they said, just because I have always needed to know what every stranger in the world thinks of me. And so I've told my people in charge of such things (don't you hate people who say things like "my people"?) to leave out the bad articles from now on. I don't need to know what Leonard Dipstick, television critic for the *Siwash Moon Ledger*, thinks of my chances in Hollywood.

Actually, Leonard, whaddya think?

Turning into a Caricature of Myself

Okay, I don't mean to turn things around again to Pamela Anderson Lee, because like I've said, she's not my archenemy. Just because she's treated me and Ray like dog poo on toast doesn't mean that I don't appreciate Pam for the very nice human being that she is.

Still, let's talk a little more about Pam, and how she's turning her whole persona into a total caricature. I couldn't believe what she looked like when she came out to host that *Saturday Night Live* episode I decided I didn't want to do. She came out for the opening monologue, like, totally naked. It was Pam being totally Pam—no irony, wit, or going against type. I mean, here she is trying to get away from that *Baywatch* thing, coming out on national television virtually nude.

She should have gone exactly against type, just have come out there and shown everybody that she was as big a geek as the dorkiest fourteen-year-old boy with braces and zits in Pottstown, Pennsylvania.

You just can't take comedy too far. It gets stupid or boring.

Pam was so into bashing me on national television that she went overboard and did everything that would have been funny too over the top. Yeah, I laughed when I saw her sniffing her armpits like I do—but she kept at it until it became obvious to the planet that this bitch wasn't out to do comedy—she was out to get me.

Me, I do it differently. I play against type whenever I can, so people can see I'm more than boobs and ass, and so that there can be a life for me out here when the implants fall and the lines come and the cellulite appears.

110

Getting Busted

I was always afraid to go on Howard Stern's radio show because I knew he'd ask me if I had breast implants, and I just knew I couldn't lie on national radio, not to Howard Stern.

I mean, how could I say, "No, Howard, my boobs are real," when everybody I've ever worked with who has seen me with my shirt off knows that I'm as plastic up there as a 32-liter bottle of Pepsi? (Of course the reason they know this is that I tell them. Like I said, that doctor in Arizona made me great new breasts, and they would fool just about everybody if I didn't have such a big mouth.)

So if I am so honest, why couldn't I say on Howard Stern's show that I had fake boobs? Because then, dopes, my mother would know the truth.

But now that I've outed myself to my mom, I'm still alive, and lo and behold, I'm not roasting in hell for my sin. I'm no longer afraid of the truth, so I'm no longer afraid of Howard Stern. Howard, take me, and have your filthy way with me on your airwaves.

I'll Wake Up

I still have this deep fear that one morning I'll wake up and discover that everything that I think has happened to me over the last three years has in fact been a dream brought on by one too many pops at nickel-draft night back on campus in Carbondale, Illinois. I'll get up and turn on the television, marveling at the amazing hangover I have. On the tube will be Carmen Electra—the original host, I learn, of this hot new show called *Singled Out*.

Then I'll realize that my dream was only a dream. At that point I would hang myself or the geek-loser boyfriend who took me to nickel-draft night last night.

tough

lost

When I left home for the first time, I was your basic confused child with absolutely no idea of what I wanted to do when I grew up. Somewhere, back in the darkest recesses of my mind, I still sort of half-assedly dreamed of being famous. Even I knew that was a pipe dream, however, so I headed off to school with the idea that there would be nothing for me in the world unless I got the college degree that my parents had always dreamed of.

My main plan for the future was that I would be a nurse. I liked the idea of taking care of people; it perfectly solved my tendencies toward codependency. To this day I still have these fantasies about pitching all this Hollywood stuff and just becoming the nurse I once planned to be. I guess I'm now convinced that I was meant to be an actress and not a nurse, but maybe in my next life.

My most physically awkward time was my freshman year at Southern Illinois University at Carbondale. I don't remember all that much of my first year at college except for the fact that I somehow managed to put on thirty pounds in only a few months.

What can I say except that I was enrolled at one of the country's most famous party schools—and that I finally had the freedom to indulge the couch potato that is my inner

MY FRESHMAN YEAR AT SOUTHERN ILLINOIS UNIVERSITY AT CARBONDALE...I SOMEHOW MANAGED TO PUT ON THIRTY POUNDS IN ONLY A FEW MONTHS.

child. For months all I did was drink beer, eat pizza, and watch, for the first time in my life, as my face, neck, and butt broke out in a mosaic of oily zits. Ah, the lures of higher education!

Unlike a lot of kids newly liberated and away from home at college, I didn't immediately go and do anything trendy like getting my hair braided or my belly button pierced. For adventure, my new friend (and now my best friend) Julie and I favored nickel-draft night at Frankie's Bar on the campus strip. Sadly, that was really my only extracurricular activity—drinking nickel beers all night at Frankie's.

Still, despite my general tameness, I did manage to stir up excitement every once in a while. The South Side of Chicago brawler inside me got a workout one night early in my freshman year when a girlfriend and I went out for another in a seemingly unending series of beers on the strip.

As will happen in bars, another woman and I happened to sit down on a bar stool at

For adventure, my new friend (and now my best friend) Julie and I favored nickel-draft night at Frankie's Bar on the campus strip.

the same moment. I wasn't looking for any trouble, but this bitch took one look at me and said simply, "Get off."

Hmm, fighting words. "No," I said.

"Go to hell," she retorted. "I'm not getting off this stool. You better get off if you know what's good for you."

Well, now. My next tactic was that barroom classic: I took the stool between my legs and pulled it back toward me. My adversary, shall we say, fell directly and hard right on her butt.

She stood up, reached for her beer, and threw the glassful of brew right into my face. What could I do but go after her in the manner I'd grown accustomed to? In other words, I had no choice but to knock her onto the floor, then proceed to thoroughly kick her butt.

The bar's bouncer, however, was not amused. He picked me up by my jeans and my hair and threw me out the door and into a mouthful of parking lot gravel. In a second, my tormentor came flying out the door too.

I'd hit the gravel so hard on my own flight out of the bar that blood was flowing right out of the top of my head. Now I was really pissed, and as that woman and I looked each other over in the parking lot, it was obvious that neither one of us was going to back down.

In a split second, I was on top of this woman on the ground, pounding away. Then she got me on my back, and it was her turn to do the pounding. With that, a gaggle of bouncers ran out of the bar and tried to separate us. Good luck.

I was so angry that I simply couldn't let go of that woman's hair. It took the bouncers literally five minutes to loosen my grip on her head. When they finally ripped me away, I came up with a big hunk of hair that I kept like a bullfighter's souvenir for about two years.

Boy, did I think I was cool. *Not!*

MY ULTIMATE FEAR

One of the things I meant to correct in college was my deathly fear of public speaking. If I ever was going to make it in show business, I knew, I had to get over my phobia about standing up in front of a class and saying, "Today we're going to talk about Theodore Roosevelt."

In high school, it was somehow acceptable to the nuns if every time I was supposed to speak in public I would instead begin sweating and hyperventilating. Now that I was in college I was determined to grow out of my peculiar habit of getting sick and throwing up every time I was supposed to stand up and talk.

So, when I got to Carbondale, I naturally signed up immediately for public speaking. And naturally the first class began with the professor saying, "I want everybody here to stand up and talk about themselves for a little while."

I tried to disappear in my seat, but the professor saw my attempt to become invisible and immediately pointed his finger at me. "Why don't you go first," he said, motioning for me to rise.

I was scared out of my mind, but I stood up. And no, sad to report, I didn't respond by giving a fabulously informative and entertaining spiel about myself. Instead, I faked an asthma attack . . . and dropped the class.

So, isn't it kind of weird that I chose this profession? Maybe not. Maybe once I conquer this fear, I'll have fulfilled my purpose in life and will die. Maybe I need to fake asthma attacks in order to live. Maybe I should go to bed.

INSANE BITCHES AND STEALING PIZZA

My college classmates were insane bitches. I couldn't stand any of them.

The worst was this woman named Rita, a skinny, perky little thing who was an absolute nightmare. Rita lived down the hall and had a boyfriend who doubled as a member of the football team. Her boyfriend was a total testosterone case who couldn't

HER BOYFRIEND WAS A TOTAL TESTOSTERONE CASE WHO COULDN'T CONCENTRATE ON ANYTHING, HE CLAIMED, UNLESS HE COULD COME OVER EVERY SINGLE NIGHT AND GIVE IT TO THE ALWAYS WILLING RITA.

concentrate on anything, he claimed, unless he could come over every single night and give it to the always willing Rita.

And so, one of my most profound memories of my life on campus was listening to Rita shrieking from the room next door, "Oh oh oh!" as she did her part to ensure that the football team won the next Saturday afternoon. Sleep, of course, was impossible; all I could do was shut my eyes and hope one of the three of us would immediately have a stroke or slip into a coma.

It was hell. I also had two sorority sister–type roommates who did whatever they could to remind me that I was unpopular and unwanted. Needless to say, there was never a question of my belonging to a sorority—I was always too broke to join.

Unlike all of my sisters, I wasn't awarded a scholarship to college. What this meant was that I had to work every horrible job that was available to an eighteen-year-old girl with no experience beyond slicing bratwurst.

So, my first year at college was largely spent dishing out Tater Tots to students in the campus cafeteria. My second year I managed to snag a gig as a bartender at Frankie's, which wasn't much better.

The men that I served at the bar were memorable for their pigginess. It was at this bar that some geek looked at my hair and asked, "Does the carpet match the drapes?"

My female customers, in the meantime, busied themselves by screaming at me. The most frequent order I heard from women was "Yo, bitch, gimme a beer. I'm thirsty!"

I also had two sorority sister–type roommates who did whatever they could to remind me that I was unpopular and unwanted.

Right away, Miss Campus Queen.

I was so broke that I really couldn't even afford to eat. Finally, I began resorting to stealing food from four guys who lived next door to our apartment. My routine for pilfering meals was pretty simple: I'd knock on my neighbors' door and say, "Yo, dudes, would you mind if I borrowed your bathroom?"

"Oh, sure, Jen," they'd always say, "go ahead."

After using the bathroom, I'd sneak into their kitchen, open their freezer, and steal a pizza. It became a daily ritual until I was finally caught red-handed. But there was no alternative for me. I know this all probably sounds like a big joke, but these were some of the hardest times of my life.

IF YOU NEED THE MONEY, SWALLOW YOUR PRIDE

Then there was my boss at Frankie's Bar. Whenever someone starts going off on the topic of how men are so much more "normal" in the Midwest, all I do is call up the image of this king of the barmaids, who tormented me during my time pushing beer to college kids.

This guy was a piece of work: He insisted that the girls who worked for him had to wear tiny short shorts and tight shirts that we tied at our midriffs, supposedly to help us get bigger tips.

Some customers liked to stand at the bar and wait until one of the waitresses came over and bent down to pick up a tray of drinks. They would just stand there, waiting, waiting, for one of us to fall out of our shirts. Jerks!

One guy's biggest jollies came when we had to bend down and grab beers out of the bar's cooler. The cooler was never fully stocked, so we had to bend down far and deep in order to scrounge up a bottle.

The whole barful of rummies would watch as we all tried to keep ourselves in our uniforms while doing our required gymnastics. It was cruel and harassing, and I really should have sued somebody's butt. But reality was reality. I didn't have any money, so I labored on and counted my tips and tried to figure out how I always seemed to get myself into these ridiculous situations.

One of the lessons you learn while working as a barmaid is the impossibility of working or reasoning with alcoholics. Instead, you deal with their messes, and if you need the money, you swallow your pride.

There was this one jerk who used to come into the bar every single time I worked. He was about fifty years old, with curly, crinkly hair, and I never once saw him enter our establishment without already being totally wasted.

He would come and stand at the bar every day, order me over to him, and then begin the next stop on his intoxication tour. The really demeaning part came when I'd bring him his order. When I was done, he would flick a five-dollar bill at my forehead as a tip.

Well, that's a lot of money, even if you have to lose all pride while picking it up. After the bill bounced off my forehead, I would do a little spin, shout out "HUH!," and bend down to pick up the dough, which I'd then stick in my little tip cup. Five bucks is five bucks, especially when you're broke.

Every twenty minutes he'd order another drink, and three times an hour I'd feel the bounce of his currency off the top of my head. I would always react the same way in an attempt to salvage a piece of self-respect.

I'd spin around once. I'd yell out "HUH!" And then I'd put his five-dollar tip in my cup.

I took his boorish behavior for as long as I could. Finally, he simply drove me nuts. I had to figure out some way to even the score, even if it meant losing a hell of a lot of money. A girl, even a broke and hungry girl, has her pride.

Finally, one night I just parked myself right next to this drunk and asked him every thirty seconds, "Can I get you another drink? Are you sure you don't want another something else?"

He didn't know what to make of how I was screwing with him. To up the stakes, I then began spinning in front of him, just as I did when he flicked his five-dollar bills at me. This time, though, I spun and spun and spun for him for free, until I was sure he was totally befuddled (and hopefully a little nauseous).

I would spin, I decided, until this guy left in search of other people and places to degrade. And finally he did, lurching out of the bar, unsure of why this obviously insane barmaid was tormenting him with an unasked-for ballet.

Don't f_ _ k with a Scorpio!

THE FIVE
WORST
PICKUP LINES

I EVER HEARD WHILE WORKING AS A WAITRESS

1 A man pointed to my hair and asked, "Does the rug match the drapes?"

2 "I think the alphabet should be rearranged so that U and I are together."

3 A man came up, reached into the back of my shirt, and pulled out the tag. "What the hell are you doing?" I asked the chump. "I just wanted to see," he said, "if you were made in heaven."

4 A jerk walked up to me and asked to borrow a quarter. "Why should I lend you anything?" I asked. "Because I want to call my parents and tell them I've just met the woman I want to marry."

5 There I was, serving drinks to campus drunks, when this guy came up and said, "Are you tired?" "Why?" I asked. "Because," he said, "you've been running through my mind all night."

THE FIGHTS, THE LIES, THE THEFT, THE END

For some reason, I kept getting into fights—real physical confrontations—while working at a different bar on campus. I really didn't think of myself as a brawler, but for some reason people were always picking fights with me while I was working.

Once I was serving this college girl, who I could tell right off just didn't like me. When I came back with her drink, she hit the bottom of my little serving tray, in the process knocking off all my money and drinks.

Well, I didn't like that very much, so of course in a second we were both rolling around on the floor beating the crap out of each other. This tussle ended the way so many of my other fights did: with bouncers or security guards picking us both up by our hair and throwing us out the door.

This fight, however, was a first. I'd never before been tossed out the front door of a place where I was working. That incident, shall we say, marked the end of my employment at that joint.

Finally, I couldn't take being a barmaid anymore, for anyone. It was so horribly demeaning that I decided that I even had to quit Frankie's Bar, where the tips were good even if the boss was a pig.

Still, I didn't know how to quit. I've always been terrible at giving employers two weeks' notice, because I just hated working those two lame-duck weeks. Instead of doing that, I'd always make up a little lie so that I could quit my job the second I wanted out.

I'm not sure why, but in order to quit Frankie's I went in and told the manager I had cancer. It was such a horrible thing to say that even now I almost start to laugh when I remember it. God, what karmic debt am I going to have to pay for telling my boss that I had cancer and had to go home immediately for radiation?

"Oh, God, Jenny, don't worry about it," my manager said when I told him the disastrous news/lie. "Just go home and don't worry. We'll pay you for your next two weeks."

So I told him I was leaving school in order to get treatment. Then, two months later, I ran into my former manager at a mall on campus. "Jenny, how ARE you?" he asked, all concerned.

"Oh," I said, "I'm fine. It wasn't cancer, it was something else." What a horrible, terrible, evil lie. I hope that by confessing it now I can get rid of some of the bad karma I sent out into the world with that whopper; I really hope that that lie won't come back to haunt me later in my life (or lives).

Finally, to make more money, I took a job for about a week cleaning the office of the apartment building in which I lived on campus. My boss, the apartment's landlord, was a real psycho who everybody called "GI Joe" because he drove a camouflage jeep and always, always, always wore combat fatigues. GI Joe was a major headcase, to put it politely.

Anyway, one day I'm tidying up the building's office when I notice a big fat wad of parking-lot permit stickers on GI Joe's desk. I didn't have a parking permit because I couldn't afford the extra bucks a month it would have cost me to leave my mother's Caprice Classic in the lot.

Actually, I would have been out of luck even if I could have afforded a parking spot. Each apartment was only allowed to have two spaces, and of course my beloved roommates had long before snarfed up the available parking permits.

So what can I say? Temptation finally got the better of me. I took a parking permit off the stack on GI Joe's desk and stuck it right on my car. No harm, I figured, no foul.

About a week passed, and I finally figured that I was in the clear. Then one day I heard an

My boss, the apartment's landlord, was a real psycho who everybody called "GI Joe" because he drove a camouflage jeep and always, always, always wore combat fatigues.

insistent ringing of our doorbell. I answered the door and found GI Joe there. He talked to me as if he were a homicide detective on a big, juicy case.

"Yes, Jenny," he said, "we're missing a parking permit from the apartment building office. You wouldn't happen to have any idea of what happened to it, would you?"

I tried to look shocked at the accusation. "I don't know what you're talking about!"

I said, trying to sound outraged. "You know, you have other people who work in that office who could have stolen it."

Satisfied for the second, GI Joe left my apartment. I, of course, immediately began to freak out. For some reason I had correctly sensed that my entire life was about to unravel.

Ding dong. The doorbell again. It's GI Joe again, back in detective mode. "Jenny, do you know whose license plate number is DCW236?"

"I have no idea," I said as innocently as I could. He left again, and this time I began freaking out in earnest. The license plate, of course, was mine, as was the car in the parking lot that it was attached to.

An hour later, *ding dong* a third time. This time, however, it was two policemen looking for me. Luckily, my roommates answered the door; I was busy in my bedroom sobbing and shaking, trying to imagine a new life for myself behind bars. I was sure I was going to prison.

"You are dead, you are SO dead," I remember one of my roommates saying to me over and over for comfort. "Those two cops are out there just waiting to take you away."

"Oh, my God," I pleaded with her, "please just tell them I'm not home. Please, I've got to think!"

She shrugged and went back to the door to tell the cops that I didn't seem to be at home at the moment. Meanwhile, I gathered up whatever wits I had left and snuck out of the apartment via my bedroom window. I shimmied down the wall, hightailed it for my car, and squealed tires as I took off out of the forbidden parking lot.

That was my last day at Southern Illinois University. I was so freaked out by my poverty, my snooty roommates, and the fact that I was about to be arrested that I didn't stop driving for hours, when I pulled into my parents' driveway in Chicago.

I was moving back home, I told my folks, and that was just the way it was. I could always get back my job at the Polish deli, I figured, and from there try to figure out Plan B for the rest of my life.

I GATHERED UP WHATEVER WITS I HAD LEFT AND SNUCK OUT OF THE APARTMENT VIA MY BEDROOM WINDOW. I SHIMMIED DOWN THE WALL, HIGHTAILED IT FOR MY CAR, AND SQUEALED TIRES AS I TOOK OFF OUT OF THE FORBIDDEN PARKING LOT. THAT WAS MY LAST DAY AT SOUTHERN ILLINOIS UNIVERSITY.

A TOTAL LOSER, ONE MORE TIME

Back in Chicago, living with my parents again after fleeing from college, I felt like a total loser one more time. I didn't have time to mope though; I needed dough. As always, I headed for the first blue-collar job I could find.

Ever since I was fourteen I'd had these crappy jobs that ranged from selling ice cream to renting videos. My first job was working at a real and authentic Italian ice cream store, where we all made the bars, dipped them in chocolate, and sold them to the neighborhood.

I lied to get that job making sundaes and ice-cream bars. I was two years younger than the sixteen I told the manager I was, but he bought it. The pace there was pretty frantic, especially during the summer, when I had to serve thirty tables at once and make all the goodies myself.

I really was a good worker; I think I only made one big mistake there. Once, while making the store's homemade whipped cream, I accidentally dropped a napkin down the blender. Well, I figured that nobody would be able to tell that a ground-up napkin was in the whipped cream, so I just went ahead and served it to the customers. Good roughage, I rationalized. What do you expect from a fourteen-year-old girl making her two dollars an hour?

EVER SINCE I WAS FOURTEEN I'D HAD THESE CRAPPY JOBS THAT RANGED FROM SELLING ICE CREAM TO RENTING VIDEOS.

Customers, of course, can be pigs. The worst revenge I ever wreaked upon someone who'd treated me like dirt in one of my minimum-wage jobs was at another in the long line of neighborhood delis where I worked.

One day I was behind the counter earnestly making sandwiches during a lunchtime rush. The line was already out the door—it was a really, really busy place, and if I didn't keep my mind on making the sandwiches, I would get hopelessly behind. My time at that place always reminded me of that *I Love Lucy* episode when Lucy gets a job at a chocolate factory and simply can't keep up with the conveyor belt.

Anyway, I was there slicing and dicing, when I heard the screech of tires braking right in front of the store. In front I saw a just-parked pink Corvette, out of which popped some blond chick with an attitude as big as her IQ was small.

She came in the door, elbowed her way up front, and said, "Excuse me, excuse me!" And then she started squeaking toward me. "I ordered a sandwich like twenty minutes ago. Where is it?"

"Don't worry, ma'am," I said, trying to be polite. "I'll get right to you and help you with your order."

Apparently, this was not the response she was looking for. "Excuse me, bitch," she said. "I need my sandwich NOW!"

No lie. That's what she said. I looked at a girlfriend, who was working at the counter with me, and she looked at me. Yes, we both realized, it was time to help this unfortunate creature with the pink Corvette.

So the two of us went to the back of the deli, where we both proceeded to spit green and gooey things out of our mouths and all over the roast beef sandwich that the princess had just ordered. We made it au jus, in a very special way. And then we wrapped it up all nice and sold it to the woman tapping her toe up front.

There's a lesson in this for all of you, boys and girls. Don't be mean to people who work in restaurants, because you never know what they're going to put in your food. For real.

DON'T BE MEAN TO PEOPLE WHO WORK IN RESTAURANTS, BECAUSE YOU NEVER KNOW WHAT THEY'RE GOING TO PUT IN YOUR FOOD.

THE POLISH SAUSAGES AND ME

And then there was the job that really defined me as a blue-collar worker—my life at the counter of a genuine South-Side-of-Chicago Polish deli and grocery store. The place was called 7–9–11, because it was open to the world seven days a week, from nine in the morning until eleven at night.

Our specialty, naturally, was Polish sausage. This was no ordinary Polish sausage that we made right there in the store. It was famous sausage, known everywhere as the best in the world. I kid you not, people from all over the country would come into the store and tell the employees that they'd come to Chicago on a religious pilgrimage in search of our holy Polish sausage. You simply wouldn't believe how I smelled at the end of the day, the fumes of smoking sausage seeping into my skin like poison gas.

Then again, my smell was probably what made all those Polish guys who hung around the store like me so much. "Hey, baby," they'd say to me, all sweet and romantic, "you smell great. What are you wearing...sausage?"

GINKOOYA

Virtually everybody who walked into my 7–9–11 Polish grocery store seemed a little bizarre to me. Maybe it was because everyone who entered spoke Polish, while the only word I knew how to say in that language was *ginkooya*. In Polish that means "thank you," which I said every time I handed over another order of fresh-squeezed pig intestines.

We sold liquor in the deli too, because for God's sake, this was a Polish neighborhood. If you know what I mean. Once again, every day I got to experience that special retail thrill of hawking alcohol in all its forms to an army of already-soused alcoholics.

I had a number of customers who made it a habit of passing out right in front of me as they tried to place their liquor order. "Hey," the drunks would say to me, "can I get

OOYA

(THANK YOU)

that bottle of . . ." When I'd look up, they'd be spread out in a pile or a puddle in the middle of the floor.

Once a guy came in with a gun and started waving it around. He turned to me and ordered, "Gimme the money!"

"Sure," I said, handing over the cash and watching with a kind of detachment as the guy ran out of the store. I sort of got used to the atmosphere of violence in that neighborhood and just forgot about it. When kids would come in groups and run out with beer, I used to just stand there and wave "buh-bye" as they scrambled out the door with the goods.

At times, even I would play the dipshit at 7–9–11. One day a guy walked in wearing sunglasses and carrying a cane. He was obviously blind, and I came out from behind the counter to help him because I'd never seen him before and he was kind of stumbling around the store as if in search of something.

When I asked him if I could help him find any items on the shelf, the man said he was looking for a special kind of cookie that was his favorite. Trying to help, I started scanning the entire aisle, looking for those magical chocolate-chip cookies that apparently came without a brand name.

I couldn't find them. Finally I looked up and asked the guy, "Well, what do these cookies *look* like?"

Oh, my God, I'd forgotten the man was blind. I almost died.

"HEY, BABY," THEY'D SAY TO ME, ALL SWEET AND ROMANTIC, "YOU SMELL GREAT. WHAT ARE YOU WEARING...SAUSAGE?"

too short
too fat
too...

While I was working at the Polish deli, I was still sort of half-assedly dreaming of a glamorous life. I somehow worked up the courage to go around to the big modeling agencies, which were all head-quartered in downtown Chicago.

I went to all the big agencies. I got the same bad story at every place I went to. I would walk in the door, sit down for my interview, and listen as some stranger told me in no uncertain terms that I had absolutely no future in front of a camera.

"Look at you," they'd say right to my face. "You're too short." Or, "You're too fat." Or, my favorite, "You look as if you should be serving beer in a bar."

This happened seven straight times. Every single time, I would leave the agency in tears. Finally, I was about to give up and resign myself to what appeared to be my life's calling inside the 7–9–11 Polish deli.

And you know what? It wouldn't have been such a bad calling. Because the people I worked with—Lou, Eddie, Mary, Stanley, Frank, Grace, and Lottie—were like a family to me.

Lottie just passed away, God rest her soul. She was a sixty-five-year-old roly-poly woman with a mustache that no one seemed to mind. Everybody loved Lottie, who could be played perfectly by an actress like Roseanne. She would have been a perfect match for my own wild grandpa.

Lottie was not ashamed to talk about sex. Sometimes she'd pick up the dirty magazines for sale at the deli and point out different facets of anatomy for our customers' amusement. She'd say, "Look at that pubic hair! That can't be real!"

And then she'd blush, then I'd blush, usually more than the customers. With me, she'd get more deeply involved in skin-magazine analysis. "Look at her!" she'd say, pointing out a model who'd caught her disfavor. "Her boobs are uneven!"

The gang at the deli was so good to me that they would have given me a paycheck even if I hadn't worked for a week. They, almost as much as my own family, taught me the meaning of loyalty, trust, and devotion.

You want to talk real devotion? Then check out their Jenny McCarthy sandwich, consisting of Polish ham and American cheese, with mayo, on a Kaiser roll. And you've got to get it *heated*.

When I was named Playmate of the Year, the only personal appearance I made in Chicago was at the good old 7–9–11 store at 4884 South Archer Street. If you need a take-out order, call (773) 847–4660. I still remember the number.

"LOOK AT YOU," THEY'D SAY RIGHT TO MY FACE. "YOU'RE TOO SHORT." OR, "YOU'RE TOO FAT." OR, MY FAVORITE, "YOU LOOK AS IF YOU SHOULD BE SERVING BEER IN A BAR."

My very first modeling picture

PLAYBOY:
THE BUNNY HOP

It is a curious but true fact that my very first job in front of a camera was taking my clothes off for *Playboy* magazine. When it rains in show business, it pours. Within a month after posing nude, I was cast in a local commercial as the television spokesmodel for a Chicago business called Frank's Auto Parts and Junkyard. With that, I knew I had arrived (just kidding).

A lot of it depends on why you appeared in *Playboy* in the first place. Many of my Playmate friends did it to get back at their boyfriends. Really. It was revenge for these girls, for some slight, either real or imagined. Others did it just because they wanted to feel sexy.

My whole attitude from my first second in the organization was that I would use this experience as a stepping-stone to something better. Coming from where I did, I didn't have a whole lot of other options.

I knew my mother would probably have a heart attack if I actually went through with it. I was scared witless by the unknown consequences of what I was doing, but I just knew deep down that it was a step I had to take if I was ever going to get out of Chicago.

To be honest, I'm not that comfortable with nudity. I don't think anybody is. Even in the take-it-all-off *Playboy* environment, I tried to remain as modest as I could.

My own very real sense of modesty is one of the reasons I've decided not to pose nude anymore. But back then, at that time in my life, I really saw no alternative.

Like I've written earlier, the day I decided to walk into

Playboy magazine's editorial offices in Chicago had started out terribly. I'd already gone to some modeling agencies in downtown Chicago that morning and been turned down by every single one of them. I was so miserable that I actually began bawling as I walked up and down the streets, going nowhere in particular.

Then I looked up at the sky and standing there before me was the *Playboy* building. There's no way I can do this, I thought, but I was drawn as if by magnets through the door of the building. It was the only way, I told myself, maybe my only chance to get to Hollywood and in front of a camera.

I was so desperate—$20,000 in debt from school on credit cards, with no other prospects except a lifetime behind the Polish deli counter. So I gathered up my courage, went into the magazine's offices, walked up to a secretary, and asked if I could talk to someone about posing.

"Honey," she said, "nobody just walks in here like you just did. You have to send in a Polaroid of yourself."

"But I don't *have* a Polaroid!" I said, all but ready to kill myself.

She must have taken pity on this poor girl with big hair whose eyes were still red from a morning of rejection and crying. "Let me see if anybody's here," she said, and soon she came back with a photo editor.

The editor, who was a woman, gave me a quick once-over and said, "Why don't you go and put on a robe and have us take a Polaroid of you?"

What the hell? So a few minutes later there I stood in this little photo studio, slowly taking off the robe.

A week later *Playboy* called me at my parents' house and told me that I'd just been chosen to be Miss October. It seemed completely bizarre to me that for once I'd beaten the odds at something. About twenty thousand girls try out for *Playboy* each year, and I'd been one of twelve picked to be a Playmate.

The next morning I went back down to the Playboy building in downtown Chicago. I went in those revolving doors as Jenny McCarthy; I came out as Miss October, a *Playboy* Playmate who, I guess, is supposed to define the ideal of modern, girl-next-door femininity. Yikes.

I WENT IN THOSE REVOLVING DOORS AS JENNY McCARTHY; I CAME OUT AS

miss october

Right off, they had me sign a release stating that *Playboy* could use any and all pictures they took of me for perpetuity. That's forever.

What could I do? I didn't know what to do or where to go. I was utterly and totally broke, twenty grand in debt with no other prospects in sight. Sure, I had my job at the Polish deli, but I could literally still smell the bratwurst ground into my hands as I looked over the piece of paper that I was about to sign over to Hugh Hefner and the *Playboy* empire.

Right off, they had me sign a release stating that *Playboy* could use any and all pictures they took of me for perpetuity. That's forever.

So I took a deep breath, looked down, and took that risk of signing on the line. I knew this was probably my only chance to get out of Chicago, make it to Los Angeles, and see if maybe I could make all those ridiculous daydreams I'd always had about being famous in a cool way come true.

I had no idea if I was going to make it—I always knew that in my mind just becoming a *Playboy* Playmate would not be making it. It had to be a stepping-stone. I knew the odds were terrible on me actually making a career I could be proud of out in Hollywood, but I figured what the hell. You rolls the dice, you takes your chances.

THE PLAYBOY MANSION

I was first introduced to the Playboy Mansion in 1993, when I was flown out to Los Angeles for my Playmate photo shoot. I was picked up by a limo at the L.A. airport and then immediately whisked away to the mansion.

After getting waved through the gates, we didn't actually pull up to the front of the big house. Instead, the driver took me around behind it, back by the mansion's guard shack. That's where they stick all the Playmates, right next to kennels, where the fifteen dogs that live on the grounds sleep.

So I walked into this little barracks and was immediately confronted with the sight of this girl lying there naked. "Don't mind me," she said, "I was just hot-waxing my poon." Hmm, I thought, I'm not in Illinois anymore.

Life in the 1990s at the Playboy Mansion is not what people probably imagine. To be honest, the atmosphere reminded me of a library. It's really quiet there now, nothing at all like the kind of twenty-four-hour party and orgy scene that most people still imagine the place to be. But it sure was beautiful.

A typical day at the Playboy Mansion usually found me waking up next to Miss December, who liked to start each morning by spreading her legs and shaving herself. Charming! That event was usually the high drama of the entire morning.

Then breakfast, very often with the chef, the nanny, and the kids. Hef's kids. They'd sit there and throw bacon at me, and I was always dying to spank them on the butt, but the nanny just smirked as if to say, "You deserve it, bitch." Can we talk about how weird it is to have two little boys dining *at home* with a bunch of Playmates? But, lest I forget, Hef was dining too—in his room. He didn't like bacon thrown in his face.

The second night I was at the mansion the phone rang, and it was the talk-show host Byron Allen asking me out on a date. "You don't even know who I am!" I said. "No way, you loser."

The next night the phone rang again. I answered and a man said, "It's Kenny." "Kenny who?" I inquired.

"Kenny Rogers," he said. And he wanted to talk to Miss December. I had to take a message—she was out hot-waxing her poon again. Thank God.

Miss December was always quite a sight with her 44HH breasts. My boobs were sort of like bowling balls, whereas hers were like boulders. I couldn't stop staring at them, they were so huge. When she lay out in the sun on her back, her boobs were so humongous that they would fall over her arms, and she'd get big white lines where the sun couldn't shine. What a sight!

Night number four? I didn't answer the phone.

Night number five there was a special buzz in the Playmate barracks. Several girls ran in, saying, "Hurry, let's go up to the mansion! There's a celebrity in the house!"

So we all went running up to the house, only to find out that the big celebrity was . . .

IT SEEMED LIKE THERE WAS REALLY NO SOUL LEFT TO THE PLACE THAT HAD ONCE HAD THE REPUTATION FOR BEING THE WORLD'S CAPITAL OF DECADENT GOOD TIMES. WELCOME TO THE NINETIES. . . .

Frank Stallone. Whoa! I was shaking in my boots.

And then, of course, there was movie night at the mansion, supposedly the most fun evening of all. My first time there I was greeted by an old fart wearing a gray Members Only jacket and khakis. He was stooped over like the Hunchback of Notre Dame, and like everybody else in Hollywood he asked me what I wanted to do with my career.

"Act," I said, like everybody else.

He handed me his card, which I later tossed in the trash. "Call me," he said. "I'll introduce you to all the right people!"

I think that was a line that actually worked in the nineteenth century, when he was still a young man. Still, he came back a few days later, humped over another inch. I think he was there for the free dinner, but he was not pleased to see me.

Out of nowhere, he started screaming at me. "You f_____g bitch!" he said. "You blew it! You'll never make it in this town now! That's not the way you treat people!" This, of course, was the line I was about to use on him.

Most days at the mansion, however, weren't so eventful. In the morning I had to call down to the big house to see if it was okay to leave my room and go work out. If Mrs. Hefner was in the gym, I'd have to wait until she was gone.

After exercising, I spent most of the rest of the day just wandering around the mansion's grounds and gardens. The spread was totally beautiful, but still kind of spooky because there was never anybody around. It was all so quiet. It seemed like there was really no soul left to the place that had once had the reputation for being the world's capital of decadent good times. Welcome to the nineties. . . .

THE BOOGER IN MY NOSE

You wouldn't believe how bizarre and surreal *Playboy* photo shoots usually are. There you are, lying on this big bed in this huge room in front of a photographer, cameraman, and fifty other guys working on the video or print versions of your naked body. It's all very uncomfortable, because the only thing you hear are people barking things like, "Okay, now roll over. Okay, now just get a shot of her butt—only her butt!"

I really had some terrible experiences with a few of the *Playboy* makeup artists. Some of them are now my best friends, but a few who worked with me on my nude shoots were truly psychotic.

One of my hardest times was when I was posing for my first centerfold. Now when you're doing the centerfold, you have to stand in your set eight hours a day for an entire week. They literally tape your outfit onto you, all to make your body look absolutely perfect. You are not to move out of that position for the eight hours they're shooting you that day, except if you have to pee. All the while you're trying to look like the sexiest thing ever invented when you're actually shaking, trembling, and sweating like a dog after a fifteen-mile run through the woods.

"SHE HAS A BOOGER IN HER NOSE,

The makeup artists, meanwhile, are in no mood to indulge your human needs. This one makeup man started yelling on the set, "She has a booger in her nose, everybody stop, SHE HAS A BOOGER IN HER NOSE!!"

EVERYBODY STOP,

And then this guy came over and literally put his finger up my nose and started digging around in full view of the assembled. I still wasn't allowed to move, you see. After that, he sent away the crew and said he needed to take a break in order to repowder me.

So the crew wandered away for a second, and the makeup artist came over to me and said, "I'm sorry, Jenny, but I'm going to fart right here, because I don't want to fart by the photographer."

And that's what he did. "Okay," he said after he was done with his digestive work, "let's all get back to work." He then walked back to his post and I was left there simmering in his foul odor.

SHE HAS A BOOGER IN HER NOSE!!"

Another makeup artist smacked me right in the face just because I dared to turn my head to see who was entering the room. Someone knocked on the door, and I swiveled an inch and said, "Who's there?"

WHAM, I got one right in the kisser. "Keep your face forward!" I was ordered. "I'll tell you when to move!"

So there I was, lying on this ridiculous Playmate set, humiliated, saying to myself, "I really need to get a better job." I just kept telling myself that it would get better, that someday this would be a stepping-stone to something bigger and better. Thank God that there was a whole new life waiting for me when I got through with *Playboy* .

> **WHAM**, I got one right in the kisser. "Keep your face forward!" I was ordered. "I'll tell you when to move!"

ARE YOU A TRAITOR TO WOMEN?

Well, of course the fact that a good girl from Mother McAuley was in *Playboy* magazine was a riotous local news flash.

I had never before done an interview in my life, and suddenly the newshounds of Chicago were upon me to get to the bottom of what they all assumed would be a sorry, sordid story of a local good girl gone oh-so-terribly wrong. Oh, and did I mention that my issue of the magazine came out during sweeps week for the local news stations?

During my very first local radio interview, the initial caller was a woman who said, "You've humiliated all the women of Chicago! You're a slut, and I hope your soul burns in hell!"

She then hung up. I figured some males would ring up to cheer me on, but every single caller was a woman damning me once again. Then things really started getting ugly. We had eggs thrown at our house. Every day kids at Mother McAuley were yelling at my younger siblings, "Your sister's a whore! Your sister's a whore!"

My mother overheard neighborhood ladies saying that if *their* daughters had done anything like I'd done, they'd have been thrown right out of the house. Meanwhile, on the local news the big local flash was "Mother McAuley girl poses nude! Details at 6, 7, 8, 9, and 10!"

That's when the phone calls from angry relatives started flooding the house. It would only get worse.

One local television station did an ambush interview of me in the Chicago bookstore where I was doing my first signing. As always I was stage-frightened, to put it mildly. Suddenly, a camera crew hustles into the store, pushing back two hundred sweating men who were waiting for me to sign pictures of my crotch for them.

Except for an appearance on the Bozo show when I was little and my commercial for the Chicago junkyard, I had never before been on television. Then here came the reporter, some very stiff corporate woman waving her fancy microphone around.

If looks could kill, I would have been dead in my chair. This reporter kept staring daggers at me as she went down the line interviewing the gathered men. Finally, she got up to the front of the line to begin questioning me.

I was so nervous that I knew I would have no control over what I would say in the unplanned interview. I looked terrible; I was wearing some cheap little outfit that I'd bought at Lerner's discount store for twenty bucks.

My hair was huge that day, the curls cascading down my head. I looked ridiculous.

It didn't help that I was wearing big, fake, Tammie Faye Bakker eyelashes and huge, bushy eyebrows that looked like they'd been painted on by Groucho Marx's makeup person. I drew a breath, the reporter introduced herself, and the red light on her news cam went on.

MOTHER McAULEY GIRL POSES NUDE!!!

DETAILS AT 6, 7, 8, 9, AND 10!

I was in such a panic that I still don't exactly remember her questions. I recall that she asked me if I thought I was prostituting myself. She also asked how I could bear to face the nuns at Mother McAuley after taking off my clothes for the financial benefit of Hugh Hefner. She then inquired if I felt like a traitor to women, if I was sending the worst possible message to little girls, and if anybody in my family was still talking to me after I'd just shamed them.

Over and over, staring at the camera like some scared rabbit in the middle of the road transfixed by headlights, I said, "I'm proud of what I did. I don't think there is anything wrong with posing nude. I'm proud of my body, and besides, all these people here are not just coming here to buy the new *Playboy* magazine because I'm naked inside. They are here because they really like the articles in *Playboy* "

It was horrible. I was horrible. This was hot stuff for the local news, and I swear

they ran that interview fifteen times during sweeps week. Sadly, they weren't awarded a Pulitzer Prize for their fine investigative work.

My life, however, seemed ruined. Now, when I look back, I'm a little older, a little wiser—and I would say the exact same thing. This time I wouldn't be reacting out of fear, but because I meant it when I said I was proud that I'd had the guts to go through with it.

THE AIRBRUSHED ME

It was totally bizarre the first time I saw myself nude in *Playboy*. What really makes me feel weird now is when someone hands me an old copy of the magazine to autograph. You see, I just don't look like that person in the magazine anymore; in fact, I never really did. I was twenty pounds heavier back then, with long platinum hair and big bangs and furry eyebrows.

When I first saw my nude pictures I thought, Wow, I really don't look that bad, I guess I look okay.

That, of course, was because of all the airbrushing they do to every single model who appears in *Playboy*. It also helps that they literally tape the clothes you're wearing onto you to give you that classic *Playboy* hourglass figure.

So my first reaction was to be amazed at the wonders of technology. But then I started fixating on the fact that the entire world was now looking at me naked. It's totally weird; it doesn't seem quite normal when strangers at autograph sessions ask me, "Will you sign on your boobies?" But what can you do?

What helped me get through the whole embarrassment thing was realizing that these pictures weren't really me. They were a *version* of me, I guess, but not a version I take very seriously.

I mean, there I was, trying to look supersexy and profoundly erotic in these pictures, and that's just not really me, or how I think of myself. That was the hardest part of the whole experience: people seeing me as this thing that I was so totally not and would never be.

So that's how I got through it. Whenever I look at those naked pictures now I just say to myself, "I was acting, and those aren't even pictures of me—they're so airbrushed that that's not even my body."

Indeed, with one turn of the airbrush *Playboy* managed to immediately take ten pounds off my 1993 figure. A lot of my relatives, however, weren't exactly buying my line of "this isn't me" reasoning.

I had bought, I thought, a few days of grace with my parents by sending them on a cruise when the magazine first came out. I actually thought there was a chance that if they were floating around on a ship they might never find out that their baby girl was showing her bare butt to the world. Oops.

While they were gone, however, I received a most disturbing phone call from one of my priest uncles. He'd read in the local paper that I was about to appear in *Playboy*, so he called me up and started screaming at me with all the authority his collar allowed.

"I can't believe you actually did this!" he began. "Your parents are going to kill you

> It's totally weird; it doesn't seem quite normal when strangers at autograph sessions ask me, "Will you sign on your boobies?" But what can you do?

when they get home. You've shamed every one of us in your family, and I'm quite sure now that your soul is going to burn eternally in hell. Where did you think posing like this would get you? This won't take you anyplace."

Yikes. All the while he was yelling at me I was thinking, Someday I'm going to show my uncle the priest. I'll show him by really making it . . . by getting to that place he said I'd never, ever be.

There were some other members of my extended family who were disgusted by what I'd done, but the saving grace was that my immediate family stuck by me like the champions they are. The six of us stayed stuck together with emotional Super Glue, and it really helped me get through all the backlash.

Now, most of those relatives who initially disowned me have finally come around, and I'm beginning to get Christmas cards from them again. That's kind of nice—I'm very into forgiveness and understanding. But I'm never forgiving my uncle the priest who damned my soul to hell. He's out.

My dear old mellow dad, surprisingly, took the firestorm the best of anybody. Of

"YOU'VE SHAMED EVERY ONE OF US IN YOUR FAMILY, AND I'M QUITE SURE NOW THAT YOUR SOUL IS GOING TO BURN ETERNALLY IN HELL."

course, at work at the steel plant, all his friends went wild when the news hit that I was going to be in *Playboy*. He handled that all really well—he brought home hundreds of copies of the magazine for me to sign for all his pals at the mill.

Thank God, though, that he never actually looked inside the magazine. If he'd done that, I truly would have been tormented for the rest of my life. I'd be in therapy deep into the next century.

Despite my protests to the contrary, the public also seemed quite convinced that this was, in fact, me lying there naked in that magazine. My very first autograph session as a Playmate was at a bookstore in Chicago, and by the time I got there, there were already a couple hundred guys in line waiting for me to sign a nude picture of myself. It felt totally awkward because I'd been gone years and years, and it never seemed like any guys anywhere wanted to wait for me for anything.

MY IMMEDIATE FAMILY STUCK BY ME LIKE THE CHAMPIONS THEY ARE. THE SIX OF US STAYED STUCK TOGETHER WITH EMOTIONAL SUPER GLUE, AND IT REALLY HELPED ME GET THROUGH ALL THE BACKLASH.

(L to R) JoJo, me, and Amy, summer 1996

WHAT IT TAUGHT ME ABOUT MEN

The whole experience really taught me a lot about men. I had to grow up in a hurry, because I was suddenly face-to-face with what most men's mentality toward women and sex really is. I don't mean to generalize about men, but from my experience, most of them certainly fit the classic mold.

I used to think there were a lot of Prince Charmings out there who were so in touch with their emotions that they wanted nothing more than to relate honestly to a sincere woman. I quickly learned that basically it usually boils down to poon-tango.

Because I had always lived so much in my inner self, it was totally disorienting to be completely judged by my outer appearance. All I wanted was a stepping-stone to Hollywood, but I always resented the kind of games I had to play to get entrée into that world.

> I was just some bimbo there to have dinner with them and flatter their egos. In fact, that was my job at these affairs—to just sit there like a centerpiece and giggle like an airhead when it seemed appropriate.

True, a lot of the girls who pose for *Playboy* love the sexual attention from men. That, however, never made me feel secure. The only way I really get that kind of inner security is when people say, "You're funny."

So, I realized, this was the game I had to play for a while to get into the club.

But those men whose unfunny jokes I laughed at and who I flattered with my attention were all fools. They were so self-involved that they didn't even realize we were all laughing at them.

Playboy used to send me all over the world just to have dinner with magazine executives, big advertisers, or whoever they thought might be able to help the publication. So I would have to fly all the way to France, say, and sit there for these interminable dinners, where all the men did was talk about how great they were.

The mentality when it came to who I was, this Playmate sitting across the table nodding mutely, was that I was just some bimbo there to have dinner with them and flatter their egos. In fact, that was my job at these affairs—to just sit there like a centerpiece and giggle like an airhead when it seemed appropriate.

But I was too smart for that bullshit; I couldn't stay awake if I had to just sit there for four hours giggling and nodding whenever these men starting telling me again what big titans of commerce they were and how their wives didn't understand them. I hated the whole idea of making myself subservient to them like that, so I just turned the whole game around.

Whenever I went to these dinners, I made this rule that if anybody wanted to talk to me it had to be about their beliefs in God. It was a good spin to put on the whole thing, but just about every time I pulled it, the whole table would get into these deep theological discussions of what God and spirituality really meant.

These kinds of little sanity-saving tricks helped make my whole term as Playmate of the Year a lot easier. For most of that year you're actually living alone in airports, taking red-eye flights to city after city and country after country, always rushing from important dinners to important lunches on another continent. The traveling is never really very glamorous, because *Playboy* always flies its Playmates coach.

Up in the front of the plane, in first class, the business executives are of course lounging in huge seats, drinking expensive champagne, and watching movies that actually won Academy Awards. Back in coach, meanwhile, I was sitting on top of people who snored and farted during the entire flight.

My tenure as Playmate of the Year was probably one of the toughest periods of my life. I'm not whining, but it's kind of hard to keep sane when the only place you can take a shower for months seems to be an airport bathroom in a city whose name you can't remember.

THE TRAVELING IS NEVER REALLY VERY GLAMOROUS, BECAUSE *PLAYBOY* ALWAYS FLIES ITS PLAYMATES COACH.

"You rock, Jenny McCarthy"

"You're a f ----- g feminist!"

ANYTHING BUT NAKED FLESH

I think I had sex only four times during the time I was Playmate of the Year. When you spend every waking second of the day posing and preening like a voracious yet innocent sex symbol, the last thing you want to do when you get home is be sexy. Instead, all I wanted to do was make some popcorn. Watch some movies. Think about anything but naked flesh.

Still, this was what I did for a living, and I had to be professional as I tried to figure out how I was going to get out of the *Playboy* empire and onto a serious career.

One little bonbon that got thrown my way was the chance to host a cable show called *Playboy Hot Rocks*, which was a music video show featuring uncensored rock

videos. My job, I was told the first day I reported for *Hot Rocks* duty, was to simply introduce the videos and interview the bands that dropped by. I'd never interviewed anybody before, and my first guests on that first show was an all-lesbian band called Femme to Femme.

There I was, with hair the height of the Eiffel Tower and lipstick caked on in layers, earnestly trying to question the band about the meaning of their music. Suddenly, while we're on camera and I'm quizzing away, a few members of the band begin to hit on me.

I panicked and reverted not to the sultry Playmate version of me, but to the South Side of Chicago girl I used to be. "Oh," I said, "you think my legs are cute."

Yah, right. Thank you.

THE LAST THING YOU WANT TO DO WHEN YOU GET HOME IS BE *sexy.*

ENVY

I'm a Scorpio, which means I have a tendency to get jealous. I'm not psycho jealous of people, but I can definitely say that I was envious of some of the other Playmates.

Okay, so I was jealous of most of the other Playmates. There were twelve of us vying for Playmate of the Year, and to my eyes the other eleven were unbelievably beautiful women who would each probably be judged ahead of me in the big sweepstakes. Despite my insecurity about my looks, though, I wanted that title as badly as any of my competitors did.

Still, most of these Playmates were my friends. It was only later, after I'd been named Playmate of the Year and then broke away from the whole *Playboy* thing, that we all stopped talking. I miss them, but I guess it's just business as usual out here in Hollywood.

My whole *Playboy* episode is kind of ironic, because I wanted that Playmate of the Year title as badly as I wanted to make a high school cheerleading team, or to have the

girls at Mother McAuley like me, or to have one normal boy ask me to the prom. Now, of course, I would never pose in *Playboy* again, even if they named me Playmate of the Century. Despite that decision, I still think that Hef is a great guy and that most of the people at *Playboy* are a pleasure to work with.

I WOULD NEVER POSE IN *PLAYBOY* AGAIN, EVEN IF THEY NAMED ME PLAYMATE OF THE CENTURY.

LESSONS FROM *PLAYBOY*

I'm still proud of having been in *Playboy*, mostly because it took a lot of guts to actually go through with it. Of course, there are times when I ask myself, "God, how could I have done that?"

But *Playboy* was my way out to Los Angeles, and the place where I learned a lot of my important life lessons and met great new friends. My new motto is to look at everything—even the hard stuff—as a lesson.

I understand that as a corporation they have the legal right to run old nude pictures of me that they own and make money off those pictures.

But at some point it seems like *enough* already!

The worst part for me is that people think I'm still posing with my clothes off when I'm not. The Christmas 1996 cover they ran of me was a doozy; it featured long-ago shots of me sitting on top of Santa.

Charming. It was weird for me to see that Santa issue, because that photo shoot had actually been one of my more surreal experiences on a *Playboy* set. I remember arriving on time wearing just a little bow, just like they wanted, and being told that there was going to be a short delay before I could hop onto Santa.

"You're never going to believe this," the photographer said, "but the Santa you were supposed to sit on died this morning."

Well, everybody was freaking out, and finally they decided to just grab this old man who was hanging around the studio and slap a Santa suit on him. Then it was my turn to take my place. Now, all these years later, those same pictures are staring down at me from the cover of *Playboy*.

So *Playboy* can have their century celebration without me. I'm done. No more. I hung up the ears and tail a long time ago, and I don't ever plan on coming out of that particular retirement.

Now, when people ask me if I liked my *Playboy* experience, I tell them it opened

"YOU'RE NEVER GOING TO BELIEVE THIS," THE PHOTOGRAPHER SAID, "BUT THE SANTA YOU WERE SUPPOSED TO SIT ON DIED THIS MORNING."

and closed doors for me. If all I wanted to be was a sex symbol, it would have been great. But I wanted more.

I wanted comedy. In that case, WHAM, the door gets slammed right in your face. This has been my battle ever since I left *Playboy*, but finally, I think, people are seeing *funny* in front of *former Playmate*.

LISTEN TO ME OR I'LL KILL YOU!

Playboy also started sending me out to my first auditions for movie roles in what appeared from reading the scripts to be highly cheesy productions. I think the very first audition they sent me out on wasn't even real — I think the producers were just some guys who knew people at *Playboy* and who wanted to hear some blond chicks read lines to them as if they were big show-biz types.

Anyway, I walked into the room where these two phony producers were, and they told me they wanted me to read like a Veronica Lake type. Now I love old Veronica Lake movies — today I could probably do a not bad imitation of her in her swooshy hairdo and cucumber-cool diction. I love how Veronica Lake was always able to talk very matter-of-factly onscreen, yet at the same time make her voice sound unbelievably sexy.

I say this all now. Back then I had no idea who Veronica Lake was. So when these pseudoproducers told me to do a reading like her, I just nodded like a dope and winged it. Veronica who?

The line I was supposed to read all sultry and smooth was "Listen to me, or I'll kill you. . . ."

I'm not sure if this translates on paper, but I read it like a truck driver who's agitated from perhaps too many thermoses of coffee: "LISTEN TO ME!!! OR I'LL KILL YOU!!!"

The producers, needless to say, looked at me as if I was a total idiot. I didn't get a callback and I didn't get the part, though I still seriously question whether any actual movie was in the planning.

I didn't feel that bad though — I had been nervous, and had had no idea how to audition or what I was doing. Slowly, I knew, I would figure out how this Hollywood game actually worked.

THE PLAYMATE STIGMA

Still, you wouldn't believe the amount of stereotyping that continues to follow my career because I was once the Playmate of the Year. At first, I quite literally couldn't get any auditions out in Los Angeles because of my résumé, and my connection to that weird world everybody imagined Hef's mansion to be.

For whatever reasons, nobody in this town wants to see a Playmate at an audition for a serious or comedic role. As I've said before, I couldn't even get an audition for MTV and *Singled Out* because of my background. My manager, Ray, had to call and bug them for a week straight before they finally said they'd give me a look.

The MTV casting person told Ray, "Fine, bring her in, we'll just laugh at her."

Well, of course there were four hundred girls at the audition, many of whom I thought were much prettier than me. But I walked into that room, acted like Jenny, and did my thing, and MTV ultimately called back. So go figure.

I knew in my soul that what got me the *Singled Out* job wasn't the *Playboy* part of me. Rather, it was the Jenny part that got me the job—the same piece of my goofy heart that had gotten me through the horrors and hardships of growing up without money and unpopular in Chicago.

I may be a little weird, but at least I've got character!

DATING RULE #1:

Fart Immediately

dating

DATING RULE #2:

Make Me Laugh

I think I'm a fun girlfriend. I like to get a little wild at times, but only at the **appropriate** times. You know that old saying about how a woman should be professional in public and wild in the bedroom? Well, that's me.

One thing you can be sure of, if you're my boyfriend, is that I'll treat you with trust and respect. One of the reasons for this is that I'm so fully aware of my own flaws that I really try to understand somebody before I judge them.

That said, perhaps my biggest flaw is the way I turn into a total psychobitch from hell when I'm PMS-ing. If you're my boyfriend during this time, please expect that I will rag on you unmercifully. I don't care what you do, it's wrong. If you buy me flowers while I'm PMS-ing, you can be sure they're the wrong kind.

Because of my tendency to turn into the creature from the black lagoon during these special days of the month, I try to make up for it the rest of the time by being a really good girlfriend. At the same time, I have to confess that I haven't had a whole lot of boyfriends, so I really don't know "the rules" on how you're supposed to catch and keep a man.

I do see, however, what a lot of my women friends do — they each dress up like a ho and think that that's the key to going out and picking up a man. Unless all you're looking for is a one-night stand, I think this is the worst thing a woman could possibly do to herself.

I really believe that you just have to be yourself and that should be enough. If it's not, screw him (metaphorically, I mean). If there is one main rule, I would say it would be to not try to be somebody you're not. And don't obsess over any one boy until it makes you nuts. Believe me, there are lots of other fishies in the sea, even if Billy doesn't appreciate you.

Just do that, and fart right away. Get everything out in the open, so to speak. Like I've said, it helps if they know the real you as soon as possible.

I DON'T CARE WHAT YOU DO, IT'S WRONG. IF YOU BUY ME FLOWERS WHILE I'M PMS-ING, YOU CAN BE SURE THEY'RE THE WRONG KIND.

RAY

Several months after Ray Manzella started managing me, he became my boyfriend. He's a great guy, and the reason I started going out with him had nothing to do with what he could or couldn't do for my career. If I had been looking to use him in that way, I would have slept with him on the first date. Wrong-o.

The main reason I was attracted to Ray, I think, was because he's a bigger goofball than me. Ray is older than me, which always interests people, but I've always preferred grown-up men who weren't into playing all the games — except Monopoly — that young guys seem addicted to pursuing in their chase for love.

You know what kind of games young guys play. If Ray and I have a fight, we talk; he doesn't give me the silent treatment the way that boys do. With Ray, there's no hanging up the phone in the middle of a conversation. Unlike a lot of the people my age that I've gone out with, he never says to me, "You're wearing too much makeup," "You're not going out tonight with your friend Mary," or "I'm not letting you go out on the town with anyone."

All that baby stuff and practiced rudeness is complete bull to me. I'm a strong believer that in relationships both people have to act like grown-ups. *Mature* relationships don't have to be *old* relationships.

I know it sounds like pure corn, but relationships have to be about growth. Both people have to grow as individuals, all the while managing to keep the love between them somehow strong.

Now it's not scientific news that women definitely mature faster than men. What all this means is that if a younger woman doesn't want to spend her Saturday nights playing Atari with a guy named Skippy, she sometimes ends up going out with older men, who know, believe me, more than just which fork to use with a salad. Ray knows what he's doing, in more ways than one.

DUMPING GUYS

I was always really terrible at dumping guys. I just never could do it. I actually haven't dumped many guys, so I don't really know all the special techniques for letting guys down without sounding or acting like a jerk.

My strategy was to always take the coward's way out. I would just avoid all their phone calls and try to just disappear from their lives. That's actually the worst thing someone could possibly do, because it just keeps the other person hanging on. And usually they hang on for nothing.

Besides being wrong, this technique is also kind of immature. Over time, I've had to learn how to break up with someone like an adult. But what do you say?

What you would like to say is, "Listen, it's not you. You're not the reason why I'm breaking up. I just kind of grew out of the relationship."

But, of course, when you tell someone this in order to break up with them, they immediately think, "What's wrong with me? What did I do wrong? How did I screw up this relationship?"

I know this because that's how I've felt when I've been told to hit the road, Jack. It's also one of the reasons I hate dating—it's just so hard to say to someone you really care for...

"It's time for us to split."

IN THE BASEMENT
WITH MY BOYFRIEND

My dad was always really good with little children, which is a quality I guess I've always looked for in a man. Sure, he's a macho blue-collar guy who's been cutting steel at the same huge mill for thirty-two years. But while he's always been big on playing the quiet and stoic manly man, he's always understood how to relate to children.

Despite how conservative and old-fashioned my folks were, they were never really into punishing us. No one ever got hit, and I don't remember ever even getting grounded. My mother, however, had a more subtle—and powerful—way of asserting control over her wild brood.

I only brought two boys home to meet my parents the entire time I was in high school, and they were both good guys who treated me well and my parents with respect. Because my parents knew and approved of them both, I was always allowed to go downstairs and watch television alone with whichever of the two was my boyfriend at the time.

Anyway, let's go back to that night when I was about fifteen years old and sitting in the basement with my boyfriend. Well, if you want to get technical, my boyfriend was actually sort of on top of me making out and engaging in a little of what my mother called "petting."

Suddenly, my mother came downstairs and totally busted us in flagrante delicto (learning Latin in Catholic school wasn't *all* boring). "Oh, my God!" I remember my mother shouting over and over, "oh, my God, OH, MY GOD!"

"PLEASE, MRS. McCARTHY, I'M REALLY SORRY, IT WILL NEVER HAPPEN AGAIN!" HE PROMISED.

Being my mother, she of course dashed upstairs and started bawling as if she'd just seen Satan ravishing her fallen daughter. I, meanwhile, immediately ordered my boyfriend to follow her up the stairs and start begging my mother for forgiveness. And, like all good boyfriends, he did.

"Please, Mrs. McCarthy, I'm really sorry, it will never happen again!" he promised.

He started crying too, and soon my mom, the ol' softie, forgave him and gave us permission to keep going out.

But by then she'd wised up, and from that point, she no longer let her guard down. From then on, my mother insisted that she had to sit downstairs with us if we ever wanted to watch television in the basement with a boyfriend. It was no longer the make-out room.

The maddest my mother ever got at me was when I worked out this elaborate lie in high school so that I could go to this party at the house of a kid whose parents were away on vacation or something. Anyway, I told my mom that I was going to sleep over at my girlfriend's house, and my girlfriend told her parents that she was going to be staying over at our place.

Then we went off to the party together, a couple of devious little twits unaware of what awaited us later that night. Oops.

Well, of course my girlfriend's father eventually figured out the whole scheme, and, after calling my parents, he came to the party at about three in the morning and dragged the two of us out of there by our hair. He then dropped me off back home with my parents, who no doubt were worrying at that time of the morning whether their daughter would ever be seen again.

That was why, I'm sure, my mother threw a chair across the room that predawn day as I walked into the house. "Stay home, young lady!" she screamed. "There better not have been any boys at that party, you better not have been necking!"

Little did she know that I was wearing one hell of a hickey. But even for this crime, she never grounded me. Like I said, I have very cool parents.

"oh, my God, OH, MY GOD!"

WHAT I NEED

There's nothing really too specific about what I need in a man. Wait. Check that. A man has to be able to make me laugh and give me respect, or there's no chance we'll make it. What good is a boyfriend if he can't make you laugh?

Sure, it doesn't hurt a man's prospects if he has a fourteen-inch…just kidding. Tell me jokes and make me laugh, and I'm yours. That's all it takes. You don't have to razzle-dazzle me or wine and dine me at an expensive restaurant. To be honest, I'd rather just get hot dogs at a stand down at the beach.

So do that, make me laugh, and treat me with respect and sensitivity. I need someone who's down to earth, and I also need someone who's a little bit on the attractive side. I don't think anyone would want to date the elephant man.

And, oh yeah, there is one other thing — all my boyfriends have to do my laundry. But these are my only requirements.

HEARTBREAK

I haven't had my heart broken in a long time, mostly because it took me so long to recover the last time from that particular form of psychic torture. The guy who did it to me was Tony, the love of my life in high school.

He dumped me after we'd gone out for a year — twelve months that I considered to be the best time I'd ever had in my life. I would do anything for this boy back then — he was the kind of guy who was on my mind twenty-four hours a day.

He was my first love, and I really believe that your first love is in a lot of ways your purest love. Maybe that's because you so trust this person — and because you haven't yet learned how *not* to trust someone.

Sadly, in a lot of ways, growing up is learning how *not* to automatically trust anybody who comes up and shakes your hand and says how happy they are to know you. You learn to do this so that you can protect yourself from the horror of being emotionally exploited.

But Tony wasn't like that. I trusted him, and he never let me down or betrayed that trust. That is, not until the day he broke up with me because he wanted "to experience other things," which I interpreted as "other girls."

Ouch! I was so hurt when he said it that I started crying, and kept on crying that entire summer. I don't think I left my room for months — the running soundtrack at my folks' house was the sound of heartbroken Jenny sobbing herself to sleep upstairs every night.

And then, after the end of that hideous summer, Tony asked me out again. I just so loved this boy that I had to go back. I was so head over heels, drop-dead in love with him that there was no question in my mind that I'd go back. He was my Romeo, and we wound up going out for another five years. Go figure. Anyway, we both eventually realized during college that it was time to separate and go our own ways. We still loved each other, but his way was toward one side of the country, and mine was toward the other.

Even though the breakup was mutual, it's a very hard thing to let go of the man with whom you first experienced true love, complete with butterflies in the stomach when he was there — and night sweats when he wasn't. It was hard to say good-bye. We kissed each other, and then said good-bye, and never spoke to each other again. There was no way we could talk to each other again; it just would have hurt too much. It's kind of weird, but we couldn't remain friends because of our shared love.

I haven't talked to him in five years, so I really have no idea what he thinks about me right now or how he's turned out. For all I know he's thinking, Jenny turned into a total ho.

I don't know. I hope not. But, Tony, if you're out there, I still love you. And I hope you're okay.

The weird thing is, every once in a while thoughts of Tony still pop into my head. I mean, I haven't even spoken to him in all these years, and there he'll be, good old Tony, remaining a part of me forever.

I REALLY BELIEVE THAT YOUR FIRST LOVE IS IN A LOT OF WAYS YOUR PUREST LOVE.

WHAT I DID FOR LOVE

Ah, all the men in my life. Actually there haven't been that many. I'm only twenty-four, for God's sake, and I still have a lot of those "good girl" lessons that I listened to from the nuns back at Mother McAuley dancing around in my head. Still, there's no question that love can make you do stupid things. I think my dopiest move for love was getting tattooed with an ex-boyfriend back in college. On our very first date, suitably lubricated at a bar on the Carbondale strip, we decided to go get tattoos of the yin/yang symbol. I got yin; he got yang.

I may have thought I was in love with him, but you just don't do that. I mean, maybe it's okay to do something like that when you're eighty and you've been with the same person for fifty years. But marking your skin forever with someone you just met is really stupid. It's not even smart if you've known him for two years. Just wait.

Okay, enough of the public service announcements. In recalling the men in my life, I think I'll start with high school. Elsewhere in my diary I've recounted my pubescent ventures into romance, and I don't feel like going back into that particular shame spiral at the moment.

Anyway, my first boyfriend in high school was Jeff. Jeff was a great guy, a real gentle and sweet person. He was also kind of skinny, a fact I never minded because I was never into steroid monsters or men with football-player physiques. I always hated those guys. Instead, I favored the quiet guys who always treated girls nicely. Even though just about everybody thought Jeff was not for me, I really liked him. He was my little Jeff. Jeff was also the first boy I almost ever slept with. I was on the verge of turning sixteen when the blessed moment nearly happened. Sadly, it wasn't so blessed.

Try as he might, Jeff was so nervous by the prospect of actual sex that he wasn't quite up to performing. For almost six months I just lay there and waited, thinking this just was never going to happen. I couldn't tell him that, of course. Instead, I opted to say over and over for five months, "Wow, this is really great!"

And then one day he almost got it in and it sort of happened. And that was it. It was over before I could blink. I couldn't believe that after all this waiting, that was it! Now I don't mean to be mean to good old Jeff, but it didn't even really feel like anything — and I guess it wasn't. Basically it was like rubbing next to a wet worm.

And then there was Tony, the love of my life for six years. See earlier for all the glorious and sad details.

After Tony came Jim, who I started to date when I was in college. He was a great guy and I really hoped it would work out — he even moved out here to Los Angeles with me when I began my life as a Playmate. Jim was so wonderful that we actually got engaged right before we moved to Los Angeles in 1993. He bought me a huge engagement rock for my finger, and I was all set to go.

Looking back, the main reason I think I wanted to get married to him was because I knew he'd be a wonderful father. We'd planned to get married out here in 1994. But then, two months before the wedding, I got nervous and pulled out.

"What am I doing?" I asked myself. "Is the only reason I'm marrying this guy is because he'll make a good dad?"

Yes. And looking back, that actually happens to be a very good reason. Thankfully, I knew enough about myself to understand that this wasn't enough of a reason to marry somebody. What I was doing by getting engaged was following the example set for me by everybody in my old neighborhood back in Chicago. Back there, a woman is supposed to get married young, have children immediately, and then just deal with the usually unhappy consequences of her early, rushed decisions for the rest of her life. Fortunately, Jim remains as one of my best friends in the world.

But then, two months before the wedding, I got nervous and pulled out.

Still, in wedding land, calling off a huge ceremony two months before the big day counts as leaving someone at the altar. I'd already paid for my dress, as had all my bridesmaids. The wedding itself had also been paid for, which meant my decision not to get hitched cost a lot of money, including the $10,000 I had put down for our reception back in Chicago.

My next relationship lasted a week. I shouldn't even count it as a relationship, but when you've had as few as I have, you count just about everything. Anyway, this guy was a musician and perhaps the biggest dork I've ever met in my life. I'm sorry if you

DORK!

eventually read this, you dork, but you were. What I remember most is that he had really long hair that reached down to his butt. Now I've never been into rocker guys at all, but one of my girlfriends was going out with the lead singer in the band the dork was in, so I felt compelled to hook up with this guy.

The dork was the band's drummer, and for about a week I hung out at this rocker guy's house in Los Angeles. He didn't even live in the house — he lived in the garage, on a futon that he spread out on the floor. Though I slept over there at the garage with him a few times, nothing ever happened sexually. Thank God. I would have died if anything had happened. This guy was just such a lazy, gross bum — definitely the most embarrassing fellow I've ever gone out with. He wasn't clingy, he was just unbelievably lame.

I remember one day in particular when I was over at his garage, and I asked him to pass me the can of Coca-Cola that was sitting on his futon. "Hey, can you pass me the can, it's right there by you?" I said. In response, he said only, "I just don't feel like reaching." Can you beat that? "I just don't feel like reaching."

I don't know why, but I've never been attracted to men who live out of a duffel bag. I like my men to keep their clothes in a dresser, have access to their own shower facilities, and have something a little more substantial to sleep on than a futon spread out on the floor of someone else's garage.

Aaach! I can't even remember this dork's name!

And then I met Ray. He's just great. And finally, I felt safe.

GAY MALE FRIENDS

I know this topic is controversial. Let's call this subject the question of "When Harry Met Sally," after the movie where Billy Crystal and Meg Ryan tried to find out if a heterosexual man and woman could remain friends—just friends—without things eventually getting weird for one of the people.

I've found that I can indeed have male friends. But I've also found that for this to be true it's far easier if they're gay. That way, not only do you not have to worry about the romance angle, but—more often than not—you've also got a terrific partner for when you want to go out shopping.

LOVE AT FIRST SIGHT

When the Wallflowers were on *The Jenny McCarthy Show* this year, a member of the cast swore she'd fallen head over heels with Jakob Dylan, the band's leader, fifteen seconds after she laid eyes on him. I wished her good luck.

Personally, I'm not an adherent of the idea of love at first sight. Not once in my entire life have I seen someone I'd never met before and decided I was in love. I just don't think real love happens that way. So while "love at first sight" might be a cute saying, I think it might be more accurate to call it "attraction" or "lust" at first sight. It all depends, I guess, on how many drinks you've had. But I don't think you can ever really call this kind of initial infatuation love at first sight. I definitely need to get to know a person for a long time before I even start thinking of seeing him romantically.

That said, I also must admit that I'm a little old-fashioned, in that a man definitely has to make the first move toward romance with me. I know there are a lot of women out there who believe in being aggressive with someone they think they might like. These are the women who decide they are going to go out and get a particular man for his money, regardless of whether or not he is seeing somebody. That's not me. I personally could never go after somebody. Believe it or not, I'm just too shy to do that. If there is a move to be made, the guy has to do it because I'm too chicken.

However, I must also admit that I can be a big flirt. So basically, I don't know what I'm talking about. But maybe I do. I certainly don't believe in that old saw about dating — if you like someone, you should be mean to him or act uninterested. To me, that is total game playing.

I don't want to play games in my relationship—I've got enough of that to deal with in my show business life. So I don't play the game of hanging up on people I really like and not calling them back for a few days just to let them know who controls the power switches of the relationship. To my mind, this is a very stupid way of going about getting a mature, healthy relationship. I think a much smarter way to find a suitable mate is to be nice, honest, and above all else, yourself.

THE PENCIL DEMONSTRATION

I absolutely hate dating. Maybe it's because of my first dating experience. I was fourteen, and Tony, sixteen, picked me up down the street. We had to resort to this subterfuge because my mother, like most of the moms in the neighborhood, forbade her daughters to start dating until we were sixteen.

Anyway, Tony picked me up in his mother's car for my first date, and we drove to the nearest mall's parking lot. We then made out there for four hours — just kissing — after which he dropped me back off down the street from my house. Charmed, to be sure.

My worst prepubescent date happened in the seventh grade. One night, a girlfriend and I decided to go over to this boy's house because his parents weren't around.

I must admit that I went over there that night planning to fool around with this boy, but I wasn't planning on going really wild.

So there we are, on his bed, making out. Suddenly, he tells me, "Stick your hand down there."

Down there? I was terrified and totally paralyzed by the entire concept of "down there." I was frightened, and not just because I didn't know what was down there.

"Do it!" he commanded me. "Stick your hand down there, Jenny!"

In response, all I could say, over and over, was, "I don't know. You're scaring me—stop it!"

Finally, he just grabbed my hand and stuck it down there. But my hand was still paralyzed; I couldn't move it. Even if I could have moved it—or wanted to—I wouldn't have known what to do. I didn't know dick back then about what to do with such things, so I just held on to it gingerly and at arm's length, like someone baiting a hook for the first time with a wiggling minnow.

My reaction, however, was not what this boy had in mind. He threw me off his bed and then ran out of his house screaming that I was the biggest dork he'd ever met. I felt totally humiliated. I gathered up my girlfriend, who couldn't believe my ignorance. "What was I supposed to *do*?" I asked her.

She told me, "You're just supposed to play with it." She took me outside the house and demonstrated, with a pencil, how to do it.

"Oh," I said. "I see. I didn't know that before."

And that was my introduction to the art of the hand job.

SORRY!

Even now, I mostly feel humiliated about the topic of dating—always have. That feeling of humiliation I had in high school, when you think everyone hates you—and when you're not being paranoid, because everyone does hate you—is still with me.

Of all the humiliating experiences I can conjure up right now, one of the worst was when this kid in eighth grade had succeeded in the make-out room of a party where no other boy had. Yep, I was going to give it up to this kid, second base, all the way. Sadly, I was wearing my usual bra that day, a hand-me-down cross-your-heart bra, probably worn by my grandmother on the day she died, bless her soul.

Anyway, this jerk-off saw me in this granny bra and began laughing. *"Look at Jenny's bra! Everybody come look at Jenny's bra!"*

I was ready to give it up to him, and instead he mocked me to everybody in the neighborhood.

I WAS TERRIFIED AND TOTALLY PARALYZED BY THE ENTIRE CONCEPT OF "DOWN THERE."

PEE IN THE BED

Maybe these horrifying early experiences explain why dating has always seemed like such a bizarre ritual to me. There is nothing normal about dating, even if you're an adult. It's totally uncomfortable, and for the first year that you're going out with someone, neither party is themselves, even if you really like each other. Instead, you're both still on your best behavior. She giggles at his stupid jokes; he opens the car door for her. You are careful even to make sure there are no food particles stuck to your teeth after meals. And then, usually after about a year, one of you farts. That tends to break the ice and from then on you're able to begin to see what the other person is really like and what you're like together in a relationship.

That's why my philosophy of dating is to just fart right away. Get it over with immediately and start figuring out if the two of you can make it. I even have an example from my own dating file where I went well beyond my commandment to fart as early in the relationship as possible.

I was once on a date in college that began with this guy and me getting totally wasted on nickel draft night on the Southern Illinois University campus. I went home with the guy afterward, though I never planned on fooling around with him at any point in the evening.

And I didn't. We just stayed up late, watched the tube, and had a little more to drink. Anyway, we eventually fell asleep in his bed, all chaste and proper and innocent-like.

I woke up the next morning and looked over to see this guy looking absolutely horrified and petrified.

"What's wrong?" I said. "Did something terrible happen?"

"You peed in the bed," he said.

That could well be the single most embarrassing moment of my life, even though it was a real good icebreaker for a new relationship.

STILL, NONE OF THE BOYS LIKED ME

It's just so stupid to try and think up things that will make a particular boy like you. Lord knows I tried when I was younger. I remember going to a party in high school where all the cool boys were drinking booze and smoking and having a grand old time.

Well, none of the girls at that party were into that, so I decided I would be the cool one and party along with the boys as if I *were* one of the boys. So I got wasted on alcohol and smoked every cigarette in the room. I even tried chewing tobacco, though no one told me not to swallow. (I puked my guts out.) And still, none of the boys liked me. It was all so stupid — my behavior that night was the worst thing I could possibly have done.

That's why I'd like to tell little girls to ignore creepy, destructive, narcissistic boys who want you to do things you really don't want to do. I so remember being young in school, listening to all the boys teasing me and thinking that I'd let them do anything if they'd just stop making fun of me. For starters, they always called me "flatlands," because I was so flat. Beyond that, they called me all sorts of other names because I was such a proper little Goody Two-Shoes. So when I say don't listen to the creepy boys, what I really mean is, just stand up for yourself.

Girls, you don't have to listen to what the boys say or do what they want you to do. Be your own person, and those boys really will like you better. And if they don't, just haul off and punch them.

CELEBRITY DATING

I really don't know what it would be like to date as a celebrity. Since I'm still dating the guy I was with when I first made it, I have no information on how famous single people meet and mate. What can an unattached celebrity do to find romance? Go to a bar and smile and flirt at a stranger like nonfamous people do? I don't think so.

I remember growing up in Chicago and thinking that celebrities dating other celebrities was totally stupid. I was sure they did that just to show us all how cool they were. Now I realize that celebrities probably dated one another because they can't really find anybody else who understands what they are going through or the peculiar pressures that a so-called star is usually under. I don't know. I hope I never have to find out.

Not that there's any celebrity out there I'd want to date, anyway. Well, maybe Tom Cruise. Physically—let's be honest—he's got a great butt. But from a personal side, he just seems like a really great guy.

It wouldn't happen between Tom Cruise and me, obviously, even if we were working together. He's married to the most beautiful woman in the world, so I can't even go in that area. The whole notion is science fiction—as in the possibility doesn't even exist except in my dreams.

Still, I wouldn't say that my dream first date would have to be with a famous hunk like Tom Cruise. Rather, my perfect first date could be with anybody at all, just as long as the man was a perfect gentleman. He'd pick me up in his car, open the door, and take me out to dinner at a restaurant I'd picked. At the restaurant, he'd let me talk the whole time. And then we'd go see a movie I wanted to see. And then afterward, maybe I'd let him take me back to his house. It would be a little house, with lots of trees. We wouldn't have to fool around for this to be my perfect dream date.

Tom

MY BIGGEST TURNOFF

My biggest turnoff when it comes to guys? Easy. I hate guys who think that they're the cat's meow and God's gift to women all wrapped together in one package. I also think that guys who wear gold chains or who have their shirts open to expose their chest-hair plantations can all just lie down and die. It's gross. Just change your style, guys, because it's never going to work!

It's also a big turnoff when a guy is overassertive about sex. Take a breather, I say. Wait a while before getting down to the serious business. Play with the hooters a little bit—or whatever—but just chill!

Out on the town, the biggest single turnoff for me is being approached by a guy who is so intimidated that he's had to get drunk to face me. That still happens once in a

THE BIGGEST SINGLE TURNOFF FOR ME IS BEING APPROACHED BY A GUY WHO IS SO INTIMIDATED THAT HE'S HAD TO GET DRUNK TO FACE ME.

while, especially when I'm home visiting in Chicago and am out with an old girlfriend.

This is sad. It's a complete turnoff. But then comes the next problem. What do you do if a guy asks you out, and you don't want to go?

Personally, if someone asks me out and has never met me before, I say, "I'm sorry, I have a boyfriend who I've been going out with for years." That's the best response. What are they going to say or do?

If you know the guy, though, the best thing is just to say, "Sorry, but I'm busy." To be honest, I've never been in this position, since everybody who already knows me knows I already have a boyfriend. My advice for young girls is to keep it simple. Just say, "Sorry, but my mom won't let me." That's always a good one.

In any and all cases, the biggest turn-on for me is a guy who can make me laugh. Give me that, along with somebody who obviously respects me and is totally honest, and I'm theirs.

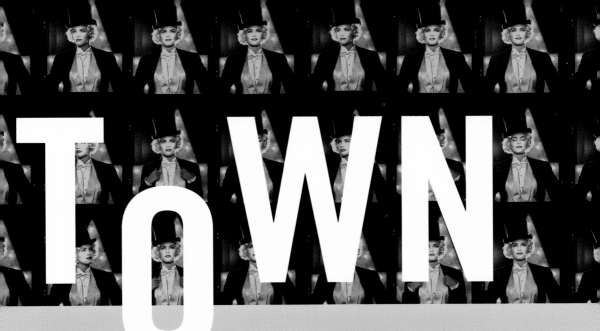

TOWN

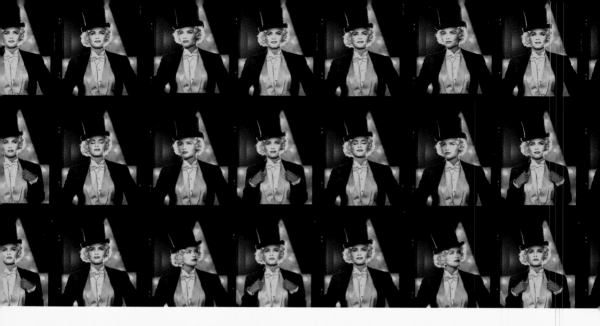

As soon as I moved out to
Hollywood, every single person
I met said I had to enroll in an
acting class immediately.
According to the official struggling actress rules, this is
what you do as soon as you get
out here: **move into an apartment; get a phone; sign up for
an acting class.**

So I asked around and heard about an acting class out in Santa Monica that was supposed to be the greatest invention since SpaghettiOs. For $300 a week, everyone in the class would be given a peek into their souls, psyches, and artistic consciences. What a bunch of bullshit *that* was.

For three months, all I did was stand at the front of the room with another actor and go through the same exercise. I would look at the other person and say, "I like your hair."

They would say, "You like my hair? Well, I like your hair. You like my hair, and I like your hair."

Then I would respond with, "Oh, you like my hair? Well, I like your hair. You like my hair, and I like your hair."

> "OH, YOU LIKE MY HAIR? WELL, I LIKE YOUR HAIR. YOU LIKE MY HAIR, AND I LIKE YOUR HAIR."

I swear, we did this every class for three months before I realized how absolutely stupid this all was. I quit and started to go out on auditions on my own, without the benefit of training. Somehow, since then, I've managed to survive.

JENNY, DON'T BECOME AN ACTRESS

I'd never told anybody in Chicago that I wanted to have a career as an actress, so no one tried to discourage me. It was only after I came out to Hollywood and announced my intentions that people started telling me that acting was the worst thing I could possibly do if I wanted to keep my soul intact and my head centered.

"Jenny, don't become an actress, don't do it!" a lot of people told me out here. "It'll destroy your personality! They'll ruin you! We like you the most the way you are right now!"

And these were friends. Even casting agents I'd become friendly with tried to dissuade me from the horrific, manic-depressive life of a struggling actor in modern-day, cutthroat Hollywood. No matter how well-intentioned they were, however, I never listened to them. Because if you know you really want to do something, you just have to keep going to prove to yourself that you can do it. And that's just what I did.

Yes, out here in Hollywood you have to put up with constant humiliation, rejection, and the power plays served up by people—mostly men—who could never get a date in high school. Those people, sadly, are now getting their revenge on the world that did them wrong so long ago by running the business of show business. (Not that I'm judging people who were unpopular in high school. Remember, I was voted "Most Likely to Go into Treatment for Addiction to Hair Spray" at good old Mother McAuley!)

And so, I did what had to be done. When I got through doing *Playboy*, it seemed that the only things I could get auditions for were movies with names like *Bikini Car*

Wash VI. Because I never slept with anybody to get a part, I was able to avoid truly bizarre scenes. Still, it's kind of weird to be twenty years old and have strangers drop their pants in front of you and ask, "Hey, Playmate of the Year—hey, Jenny, would you mind signing my butt?" And look at me now—just as big a geek as ever, but with my own network television show!

So, even though you don't have to be sleazy to get ahead in Hollywood, I definitely think you need a competitive spirit. This business is really horrible when it comes to competition and its evil stepsister, jealousy. I try to stay away as much as I can from that world of jealousy and envy, but sometimes you just can't escape it (especially if you're a Scorpio). And though there really aren't any rules to making it in Hollywood, I'd say that if you don't have a lot of competitive blood inside you, you simply won't make it.

That said, just being competitive and warriorlike isn't nearly enough to make your mark. You have to use your competitiveness to make yourself do a better job. Doing a better job than the competition is the key to making it in this town. Hollywood loves only one thing more than toasting winners when they're up, and that's kicking so-called losers when they're down. Tough place, this town—but I've always known I'm tougher.

SEE JANE RUN FROM DICK

One of my first auditions was for a pretty major part in a Steven Seagal film called *Under Siege II*. After doing five different auditions for the part, I was notified that I had made it to the final casting call. It was time, I was told, to read with his highness Steven himself.

When I got to the audition, I was seated in this room with ten women who looked exactly like me, except they all had puffier lips. Everyone just sat there reading magazines and pretending not to notice one another.

The actresses all went in, one by one, and the hours crawled by. Finally, Steven Seagal came out, looked at me, and said, "You must be the last one. Come and follow me into my office."

So I did. It was a pretty strange place—he had shag carpeting and a huge dead bear that dominated the room. There was an enormous fireplace and these big puffy couches. Very Hollywood big-shot decor.

"Why don't you have a seat right there on the couch?" he said. I sat down.

"Now you know," Seagal said, "you can get a little closer."

Yeah, right. I was supposed to read about five lines with him, and I tried to focus his attention back on the script before us. "Okay. Would it be all right if we just read now?" I asked.

But he wasn't ready yet. Instead, he kept talking. He told me all about his time spent living in Asia. And then he launched into this sermon about how he had managed to cleanse his soul and all that kind of Warrior of the Far East crap.

> And then he launched into this sermon about how he had managed to cleanse his soul and all that kind of Warrior of the Far East crap.

Finally, I'd had it. "Listen," I said. "Let's read the lines." So I stood up and got ready to read my lines. But before I could start he interrupted.

"You know there's partial nudity in this," he said.

"No, there's not," I said.

"Oh, yes, there is," he insisted. "And I can't really tell what your body looks like for the part."

I immediately went into shock. Then I got pissed. And when I get angry, I have a tendency to start yelling. "You know what?" I screamed. "Why don't you just go out and buy one of my *Playboy* videos for $14.99?"

And then I stormed out. But Steven wasn't through with me yet. He followed me back to my car and said, "You better never tell a soul."

Oops. Sorry, Steven.

Probably the worst thing about the whole sordid Steven Seagal episode occurred after I got home and called my manager to report what had happened. "How could you send me out on that Steven Seagal audition when you know I'll never lie down for a part?" I asked him.

"I'm sorry, Jenny," my manager said, "but I didn't really know if you would lie down or not."

Wrong answer. Wrong manager.

And that's when I decided to let Ray Manzella take care of my day-to-day management responsibilities. He started managing me and made those all-important calls to MTV reminding them that this Jenny McCarthy was no Playmate airhead and that they really owed it to themselves to check me out for the co-host gig on their new show *Singled Out*.

DAVID LETTERMAN

Probably my favorite talk-show experience I had during the time *Singled Out* first hit was on *Late Show with David Letterman*. A lot of shitty things are said about David, but I think he's a cool guy.

I always get very nervous when I go on any talk show. I'm still frightened by the prospect of public speaking, and going on a program where you know the host hunts heads is a little daunting. I was especially scared of going on the Letterman show because David is so sarcastic. It's no big trade secret that his basic on-air strategy a lot of the time is to make the celebrity he's interviewing look like an idiot. While I enjoy watching this in the privacy and comfort of my own home, the idea of sitting in David Letterman's hot seat paralyzed me with fear. Still, the show must go on. All I could pray for was that David wouldn't go out of his way to make me look like an ignorant bimbo.

The only thing I remember about my introduction that night is standing stiff as a sequoia behind the curtain as the announcer called my name. With that, I walked out onstage, waved to the audience, and sat down. When I looked up, David Letterman was sitting a few inches away from me rapidly flipping through the pages of my last pictorial spread in *Playboy*.

It was obvious that he was trying to fluster me, and it was working. Still, I got up the gumption to save myself and resorted to that old Jenny McCarthy strategy: When in doubt, yell.

"Hey, Dave!" I barked at him, pointing up to my head. "My eyes are right up here!"

The audience hooted and howled in delight, and David was a sport. He tossed the magazine over his shoulder, looked me straight in the eye, and conducted the rest of the interview like a perfect gentleman. I respected him a lot for that.

"HEY, DAVE, MY EYES ARE RIGHT UP HERE!"

THINGS TO DO IN DENVER
WHEN YOU'RE DEAD

Finally, all my efforts at auditioning for a serious movie role paid off. The name of the picture was *Things to Do in Denver When You're Dead*, and it sounded at first as if I'd landed a cool role in a funky film.

My part was as Christopher Walken's nurse. Christopher Walken played a paraplegic in the movie, and in my three scenes I was supposed to take care of him and interact a little with Andy Garcia. I didn't have any lines at all except at the beginning of each scene, when I was supposed to say hello to Andy.

"Hello." Cut. "Hello." Cut. "Hello." Cut. You get the idea.

The most memorable part of making this movie was how bad Christopher Walken smelled. I mean, years spent behind the counter of a Polish deli had trained nothing if not my nose, and let me tell you, Christopher Walken *really* smelled bad.

And, of course, I had to spend ten hours a day sitting next to him as his on-screen nurse. I don't know quite what to compare his smell to, except that he was rank. He had a kind of essence of formaldehyde coming off him. The experience gave new meaning to the idea of suffering for your art.

> **✳ Years spent behind the counter of a Polish deli had trained nothing if not my nose, and let me tell you, Christopher Walken *really* smelled bad.**

Our first day of shooting started at seven in the morning. Right before we began, Christopher removed an apple from his pocket and took a bite. Now it was time to rehearse, and the apple had to disappear. All at once, every stagehand yelled, "Do you want to give us the apple, Christopher?"

"No!" he said, as he shoved the apple back into his pocket. Christopher was then strapped into his wheelchair and he got ready for his scene. At the end of the take, he got unstrapped, popped up, pulled his apple out of his pocket, and took another bite.

This went on, take after take, for ten hours. By the end of the day, Christopher

Walken still had that damn apple, which was then brown, oozing, and utterly disgusting. During each break, though, he insisted on pulling out the mushy core and taking a chomp out of it. Sometimes, in my darkest nightmares, I can still hear the sound of Mr. Walken's apple.

There was, however, a plus side to these two weeks of torment. During that time, I got to stare at Andy Garcia's butt all day long. Andy didn't really speak to me the entire time we filmed, yet in his way he helped me through my trying first time in the wonderful world of independent film.

SHOWGIRLS

Probably my goofiest audition ever was for the lead role in *Showgirls*, that big-budget movie about strippers in Las Vegas. The movie totally tanked, so I'm really glad I didn't get the part. Not that there was ever a snowball's chance in hell that I would have. I really didn't want it anyway, but this was early in my career in Hollywood, and my management thought it would be a good idea for me to read some lines before some real Hollywood producers and directors.

So I headed off to the *Showgirl* auditions, and I actually got called back five times for the lead role. At my final callback, I got to read for Paul Verhoeven, the way hip director who would ultimately be blamed for the debacle this movie eventually became.

"Great!" the famous director said after I'd read my lines for him. "One last question," he asked. "Can you dance?"

I knew he meant exotic dancing, stripping, what-have-you. And to his question, a simple no would have been the truthful answer. But I totally lied and told him yes, I knew how to dance.

It was actually sort of a half lie, I figured, since I used to be a cheerleader in high school. I mean cheerleading is a dance art form, isn't it? It's kind of like stripping, no?

"Yes," I told the director one more time for emphasis. "I know how to dance."

"Good," the director said, pleased to hear that apparently I knew the difference between a touchdown cheer and lap dancing. "Because the last test is a dance audition, and you have to go."

Okay, I told myself, I can do this. And on the appointed day I showed up at this fancy Hollywood dance studio all decked out in my sweats, cap, Nike gym shoes, sports bra, and proper peppy attitude. "Whooo!" I yelled as I bounded into the studio. "Yeah, I'm here!"

What a dope I was. The wind went out of my sails when I saw who my competition was—and what they were wearing. Spread out before me in the studio was a collection of professional dancers decked out exclusively in fishnet stockings, G-strings, and their little dancing shoes.

Okeydokey, I thought, so I look a little different than these women. That's okay—I'm Jenny, and that will be enough. I hope.

Then a choreographer came out and told us we'd have fifteen minutes to learn the dance she was about to teach us. "All right, girls, line up," the choreographer ordered. "Five, six, seven, eight!"

And then she was off, demonstrating a hysterically cheesy sex dance favored in a Vegas lounge show. Still, I was really proud of myself, because I was actually able to learn the dance in the allotted time.

After practicing, all the women were ordered to the back of the room, from where we would be summoned one at a time to do our prerehearsed shimmy. I was fourth, and I was shaking with fear as I approached the table where all these producers of the film were sitting like kings.

"Ready?" said one to me. "Do the dance! Five, six, seven, eight!"

Boom, boom, boom went the music, and I actually did the dance exactly as I'd been taught. Another small victory for scaredy-cat Jenny.

The producers liked it too, I guess. After conferring among themselves for a little while, they turned back to me and said, "Okay, now we want you to do a dance that's your own. We'll provide the music, and you just dance however you feel."

Well this was a surprise. I wasn't expecting

to do my own little dance. I didn't *have* my own little dance. But that was okay too. I was a professional, I reminded myself—or at least I wanted to be.

Boom, boom, boom, on comes the music, and I started moving like I used to on the dance floors of the Carbondale, Illinois, campus bars. Pretty good, I thought, not too shabby.

The producers, however, were not impressed for some reason. Within two seconds of the start of my own dance, their faces had all fallen like a bad soufflé.

"Thank you very much," one of the producers said to me, barely bothering to give me the "blahblahblah you're really great" courtesy speech you usually get when you've totally not gotten a part. As I headed out, I still couldn't figure out exactly what had gone wrong.

"How'd you do?" all the auditioning girls asked when I got back to our little holding pen. "It was really weird," I said. "I was fine on the rehearsed dance, but I didn't know what to do with the part where you made up your own dance."

Now I'd confused the girls too. "Show us what you did," one of them asked, looking for tips on what not to do.

So I did my little Midwest, big-haired teenager dance, and their jaws dropped just as the film's producers had. "Oh, my God, how could you have been so stupid!" one of them said to me. "You were supposed to *strip* for them! This audition is for *Showgirls*, not your high school prom!"

WITHIN TWO SECONDS OF THE START OF MY OWN DANCE, THEIR FACES HAD ALL FALLEN LIKE A BAD SOUFFLÉ.

Oops! There I was, doing the Snake or the Swim or the Hustle or whatever, and I was supposed to be taking off all my clothes and shaking what was there for the perusal of the producers.

Oops, indeed. Still, this is my favorite auditioning story, just because it's a little shot of innocence in a world full of casting couches and sleazy tryouts. Better then anything, though, I guess this episode shows where my mentality was at the time. You can take Jenny out of the South Side of Chicago, but you can't take the South Side of Chicago out of me.

LOVE SCENES

Despite what everybody thinks, I'm actually quite modest, and I have a lot of trouble doing love scenes on-screen.

Every time I get a promising-looking script I just pray that there aren't love scenes. I've had to do two or three of them, and I've got to say they are the most uncomfortable scenes that I can imagine doing as an actress. It's horrendous, standing in front of a crew half-naked, totally making out with some guy while fifty people lurk behind the cameras watching you do it. After doing that a couple of times, I had a new appreciation for actors and actresses who can actually make you feel their passion when they're doing a love scene.

To me, it's totally unnerving. I don't think there's one person I'd actually want to do a love scene on screen with. Okay, in my dreams, maybe Tom Cruise. I know, I know, I'm a geek for picking Tom Cruise. But confess, women; how many among you *wouldn't* want to do a love scene with Tom Cruise?

HARD WORK PAYS OFF

Movies, however, were not to be my lot in Hollywood. At least not right away. There would be no time, not after I was chosen to be the co-host of MTV's *Singled Out*.

One of the very best days of my entire life was the day I found out that I'd gotten the part on *Singled Out*. I thought the auditions would never end—I had to try out sixteen different times over a two-and-a-half-month period. The audition process for that show was so grueling that by the end of my last callback I was lying on the floor, bawling my eyes out.

I just couldn't take it anymore; the pressure, the stress of not knowing, the feelings of worthlessness I knew I'd feel if after all that effort I didn't get what I wanted. And then, as soon as I got home that day, the phone rang.

"Congratulations," said the voice on the other end of the line. "You're the new co-host."

That was so great. Beyond the ego gratification of being chosen out of I don't know how many hundreds for the role, it was also proof to me that hard work truly does pay off. I know that sounds corny, but that really is the lesson I'd like to impart to all the young boys and girls out there. Just keep trying, and your dreams will come true. But you have it to give it all your time, effort, and soul.

GO! GO! GO!

People are always asking me how I kept my energy at such a nonstop manic pace on *Singled Out*. It wasn't easy, let me tell you.

Most people actually assume it was a pretty cushy job working on an MTV game show. Just about everybody I met thought I was at the studio about an hour a day, filmed that day's show, then got to go home.

Wrong. In television—and especially on the cable networks like MTV—you have to

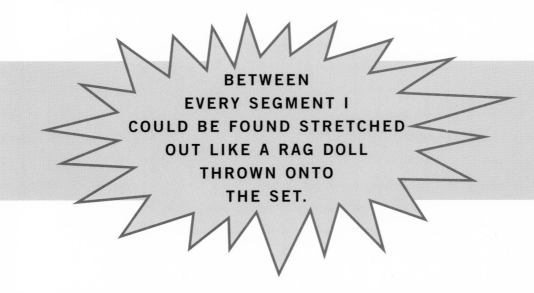

BETWEEN
EVERY SEGMENT I
COULD BE FOUND STRETCHED
OUT LIKE A RAG DOLL
THROWN ONTO
THE SET.

film a number of shows a day to keep costs down. On *Singled Out* we filmed four shows a day. Each day was twelve hours, and not a second was wasted while everybody ran around trying to make the show work.

For most of those twelve hours I would be sprinting harder than everybody else, shouting just about every second of the way. There were a lot of times when I just didn't have the energy, but there was no alternative.

Every time the camera light was on it was my job to screech out witty and not-so-witty encouragements or disses to the contestants. When I wasn't provoking everybody, I was just supposed to bounce around yelling, "Yeah! Right! Go!"

But as soon as that red camera light went out, I would collapse wherever I was and just rest. Between every segment I could be found stretched out like a rag doll thrown onto the set.

If you've seen *Singled Out* at all, you know that I spent the last five minutes of every show jumping around, shrieking, and pounding people. From that, most people seem to assume that I'm this incredible storehouse of energy. I'm really not—I have just as much energy as anybody else. I've just learned how to *conserve*—and then go wild when that light comes on.

A lot of people have asked me if that was the "real" me out there on *Singled Out*. I always tell people that yeah, in a lot of ways that is, in fact, really me. That was what was so great about MTV—they hired me for my personality, then allowed me to let it all come out on-screen. It was me with the volume cranked up high, and then maybe one notch higher. I was on eleven, in a *Spinal Tap* sort of way.

Normally, I'm a little more animated than the average bear. I talk with my hands a lot and emote in my everyday life. However, I don't walk down the street telling guys, "Dude, you're a babe!" I don't normally pinch people's butts or beat them up when I'm on line at a store.

But when you're onstage with a hundred screaming, sweating, love-hungry young people, you're bound to act a little crazy. Especially when a certain proportion of those people are young men trying to pinch *your* butt. When someone does that to me, whether I'm on-camera or not, you just know I'm going to punch them right in the face. Isn't that only justice?

CHRIS HARDWICK

One of the most frequent questions I'm asked about *Singled Out* is about my relationship with the host, Chris Hardwick. For some reason, a lot of people think that we dated (did anybody ever wonder if Monty Hall on *Let's Make a Deal* was going out with Carol Merrill?).

Well, I never did go out with Chris, but working as intensely as we did with each other for twelve hours a day meant that we shared a lot of exciting and tense moments. After a while, we became sort of like a brother and sister. And like all brother-and-sister combinations, our relationship had its ups and downs. But most of the time, if I came into his dressing room crying about what was going on on the set, he'd console me—something that can be done without having sex.

Now that I'm gone from the show, I really do miss the energy of being onstage with a hundred young people screaming, "Yeah, I want a date!" What I definitely don't miss, however, are the guys who used to grope me while I tried to keep them penned in, and the guys who thought they would prove how cool they were by being mean to me. My favorite guys were the ones who just thought they were SO COOL—they were so easy to make fun of.

There was another reason I could be so mean to the boys on the show. People didn't see what happened when the camera was off, when guys would yell at me, "Hey, Jenny,

"HMM, HE'S A CUTE ONE WHO I COULD SEE GOING OUT WITH."

I've seen better legs on a table." Uh-huh. I mean, it could be horrible. So while I miss the excitement of the show, I most definitely don't look back with fondness on all the pervertedness I was exposed to. When there are fifty testosterone-soaked guys jumping up and down all around you, you can be sure at least half of them are rude, inconsiderate dorks.

Only once was there a contestant on the show who made me think, "Hmm, he's a cute one who I could see going out with." I actually tried flirting with him during the game, but it didn't really work. I think he thought I was just doing my normal on-camera shtick of alternately flirting or beating up the boys and that he was lucky enough to be one of the guys I was nice to. The weird thing was, he was the one boy out of the fifty who won a date on the show. I was sure he wouldn't win, just because of the harsh mathematics of *Singled Out*, but he actually won, fair and square. Not that it mattered, of course. I already had a boyfriend, so it wasn't like I could do anything anyway.

Mostly, though, I was too busy making an on-screen spectacle of myself to spend any time thinking of anything—or anybody—else. It was work, but I always tried to make it fun.

I always thought it was funny to see people's reactions when I'd blow a fart in front of fifty guys onstage. That never seemed weird to me, because I'm pretty comfortable, as you know, with my bodily functions. My friends know me and by now view this as normal. But those guys on the show would be utterly flabbergasted that I would actually dare to fart in front of them. What can I say? That's just me. And the same goes for picking my nose. This isn't an act. Because you know, there's only so much nose blowing one can do. Sometimes, if something is stuck up there, you have just got to go in and get it.

Despite my apparent immodesty, people on the show still found ways to embarrass me. The worst thing that ever happened to me on *Singled Out* naturally involved my always rebellious digestive system.

Ever since I've been little I've been clogging toilets. I don't know why God has cursed me this way, but I've come to accept the inevitable embarrassment. This particular time, though, was too much. There was a break on the set this one day, so I ran back to my dressing room and did what people do. Of course I clogged the toilet, and within seconds it had overflowed and was flooding my dressing room. Charming.

So I called for help. And fifteen seconds later, over the loudspeaker placed in front of three hundred would-be contestants, everyone heard a disembodied male voice announcing, "Jenny McCarthy has clogged her dressing room toilet. We need maintenance people and somebody with a plunger to go to her dressing room immediately. Repeat, this is an emergency, Jenny McCarthy has clogged her toilet!"

So you think that nothing could embarrass me? Believe me, just remembering that incident sends me into spasms of shame. Yikes!

"HEY, JENNY,
I'VE SEEN BETTER LEGS ON A TABLE."

FAME

I STILL BLAME IT ALL ON...

BOZO

I'm pretty sure I know what my life would be like now if I hadn't chased my dream of becoming a show business legend (or at least a working actress). I would still be living in **Chicago,** and I'd be **married** with at least one **baby** by now. Maybe I would have tried acting later on, when my **kids** were grown up a bit. But I probably would have ended up as just another blue-collar **housewife** struggling to pay the bills, feed the **family,** and keep shelter from life's storms.

I doubt I ever would have gone back to finish college, because I'm sure I wouldn't have had the money. Money. While I'm not sure it's truly the root of all evil, it does certainly change everything.

So far, money has mostly changed things for the good. Growing up, I became accustomed to always being broke and to always, always, always eating leftovers. I can't even begin to explain the karmic high I got when I was finally able to support my family and pay off their bills. Helping my sisters get through college also felt great . . . as did knowing I could afford all the things I ever wanted but could never pay for before (within reason, she added, knowing her accountant would be reading this with the same attention he gives to her checkbook).

"YOU, LITTLE BLOND CHICK. DO YOU WANT TO HELP US OUT?"

"OKAY."

The first time I ever felt like a star happened when I was in the fourth grade. I'd been chosen to sit in the audience during a taping of *Bozo the Clown*, that classic clown program that came out of Chicago. I remember standing in line in my Girl Scout uniform with the rest of the audience waiting to get in when this guy who worked for the show came out and said, "We need somebody to read a cue card on the program."

Everybody was going nuts in line trying to get this guy's attention. "Pick me, pick me, PLEEEZE pick me!" all the little kids shrieked, throwing their arms up into the air. I, as per usual, was so frightened that I couldn't even raise my hand, let alone yell out at the producer.

"Pick me, please," I said silently to myself.

The Bozo guy must have been able to feel my silent plea, because he looked at me and said, "You, little blond chick. Do you want to help us out?"

"Okay," I said, squeakily.

With that, I stepped over the line, both literally and figuratively. I was in show business. The producer took me backstage to meet Bozo, and we practiced for a little bit. My job was to take the microphone, look into the camera, and say, "Learn how and why, next on *Bozo the Clown*."

If I do say so myself, I did a swell job on-camera. Even Bozo was impressed. "You're going to go somewhere," the famous clown told me. And look—I actually did. Anyway, that little spot ran for thirteen weeks on television in Chicago. I was a star! Unfortunately, my family couldn't afford a VCR at the time, so we never got to tape it. It was kind of sad, because I never got to see me doing my little line again after those first thirteen weeks.

Still, that was my beginning. And ever since, show business is all I ever wanted to do. Though I went for years without admitting it to anybody, I can now finally reveal the truth.

I got the showbiz bug from **Bozo.**

F R A N K ' S   J U N K Y A R D

Fame is such a relative thing . . . at what point is one truly famous? Being on *Bozo* in fourth grade made me feel "famous"; so did doing a commercial for Frank's Auto Parts and Junkyard back in Chicago in the days when nobody really wanted to take a look at me.

After many, many turndowns by every single modeling agency in Chicago, I finally was signed by a teeny company that thought it could find me some local work. I was psyched, because all I wanted to do was get in front of a camera and get some tape of me for a reel.

What they came up with was Frank's Junkyard, which was just fine by me. The ad ran for years at two in the morning in Chicago; in it, I stand there with my big hair in front of a picture of the garage and say simply, "Do you want big money? Sure you do. Then why let someone tow your car away without giving you big money? Don't do it. Call Frank's Auto Parts and Junkyard in Chicago."

That was the entire commercial, and I hear it's still airing. So if you're an insomniac and in Chicago, tune me in and see my blastoff to fame.

My second local commercial was for a restaurant called Dappers, a Chicago family diner renowned for its terrible food. My job was to sit in the restaurant while real live families supped around me and plug the delicious cuisine. "Are you tired of fast food?" I asked the camera. "Then try Dappers. Dappers East of Chicago."

Welcome to show business!

SITTING ON THE CAN FOR CANDIE'S

I still can't believe what a fuss it caused last spring when on behalf of Candie's shoes I posed perched naked on the toilet, my underwear down around my ankles. Yes, I guess I was pushing the envelope here, but it was a joke! It was funny! Laugh!

I wasn't self-conscious about posing on the toilet; as I've mentioned, it's my natural habitat. Candie's was simply playing off my wacky MTV character in an attempt to capture the attention of younger people.

I don't want to get defensive here, but why doesn't it cause a stir if it's a man shown sitting on the can? How come Jim Carrey can do a man on the toilet in *Liar Liar*, and it's just funny, but if a woman does it, it's an advertising scandal?

Why not just laugh?

HEY, LOOK—IT'S HER

For about the last year or so friends have told me that I've sort of turned into the queen of the Internet. There are a couple dozen web sites devoted to me, I've heard, but so far I haven't seen any of them.

I don't really like even knowing about all this stuff. This is because I've also been told that the bulk of the information floating out there on the information superhighway relates to my *Playboy* years, complete with computer-ready copies of those nude photographs I posed for all those years ago and even pictures of me with my face and someone else's body twisted into some pornographic scene.

I do, however, go on America Online sometimes. I've visited some chat rooms there and have even been brave enough to go into a place called the Jenny McCarthy Room. Whenever I've gone in there, I've told the people in the room who I was, but nobody believed me. Instead, all the guys in the Jenny chat room would begin calling me names and throwing insults at me. Just like high school! I wouldn't believe me, either. But it was still fun hearing what they had to say.

I even mostly like it when adult fans come up to me in public to say hello and share

"YOU'RE THAT CHICK!"

a moment. True, people don't really react to me as if I'm a real person; there's something about being on television that makes people think of you as not really human. Still, it's pretty fun to have cashiers look up from making me change and shout out, "Oh, my God, dude, you're that chick!"

No one ever really does that to me in Los Angeles, because everyone is so concerned about never looking starstruck. Either that, or because nobody here in Hollywood really gives a crap who you are.

Arnold Schwarzenegger could walk down the street in Los Angeles and people would just mumble, "Ah-nold." As I've said, it's very important to seem unimpressible out here.

But when I get out of L.A. and go to Las Vegas or Chicago, people sometimes go nuts when they see me. I must admit that it takes a little while to get used to people following me and screaming, "Hey, can you punch me?"

It's not just men who do this. Take what happened not too long ago when I was peeing in a public stall in Chicago. All of a sudden, a woman's head popped over the divider from the stall next door.

"You're really her, aren't you?" she said as I went about what I was doing. "Come on," she continued, "tell me what it's like. Tell me *everything*."

Some other time, if you wouldn't mind. Still, it's always kind of nice when strangers come up to me and say, "I enjoy your work."

Once in a while, though, things can get a little hairy. Last winter I was Christmas shopping with my sister in Los Angeles when we had a little drama. We were walking back to our car and talking when suddenly I realized there was a bunch of giggling kids behind us.

"Who's following us?" I asked as I wheeled around. There, in front of us, were about ten twelve-year-olds screaming, "It's her! Look, it's her! Hey, I think it's really her! Do you think it's her?"

I was kind of going *uh-oh*, because there were ten of them, and you never really know what's going to happen when you've got a little gang in front of you. My sister and

MY BEST FRIEND, JULIE, IS ACTUALLY THE ONLY PERSON I KNOW WHO'S EVER BEEN COOL WITH ME WHETHER I WAS FAMOUS OR NOT.

We got in the car, which in seconds was engulfed by little kids pounding on the windows and yelling, "Hey, it's the love chick! C'mon, open the door and sign this piece of paper for me!"

I got kind of scared, and we literally did a hundred-yard dash to the car.

We got in the car, which in seconds was engulfed by little kids pounding on the windows and yelling, "Hey, it's the love chick! C'mon, open the door and sign this piece of paper for me!"

Well, we didn't. I had to drive away. I'm sure those kids thought I was a total bitch, but I was just too nervous to let them in.

In fact, if there's a single misconception that people have about me it's probably that I'm a bitch. I'm really not, but if I stand outside myself I can understand why a lot of people might think that I am. If I detach and watch myself acting out on television, I can see how some people might think, "Who does that girl think that she is? She's not funny—she just thinks she's cool because she's on MTV."

Yes, that might be how I appear. But I also realize that you really have to get to know people before you make those kinds of judgments. Still, people do judge, especially after you become successful.

Without sounding whiny, fame can really separate you from people. My best friend, Julie, who lives in Chicago and whom I met at college, is actually the only person I know who's ever been cool with me whether I was famous or not. She's the only one I've known from my entire life who treats me like an equal friend, no matter what my circumstances are at the time. What I love about her most is that she's always treated me exactly the same way, whether I was on television or not.

Still, I never really try to star-trip at all. Only once did I wear a disguise in public, and the results were just ridiculous. I was going to Las Vegas, where I like to go to relax, and brought a red wig with me so I could avoid the people who always hound me when I'm out there. The only problem was that I was still recognized.

The reason I had to resort to what boxing promoter Don King calls "trickeration" is because I like to gamble a little to unwind. And I tend to lose a lot of money when I'm being hassled in Las Vegas, because it's hard to pay attention to your blackjack hand when all night long guys are coming up to you drunk, slurring and saying things like, "Hey, my friend used to date you!" Yeah, right!

This time in Vegas, though, for the defense of my pride and bankbook, I brought

along that wig. It didn't work, and I was totally embarrassed. I mean, there I was, playing blackjack in this ridiculous red wig, and all night long people were still coming up to me and going, "Hey, Jenny, can I have your autograph?"

Maybe I blew my own cover when I kept making faces as I watched my chips come, go, and come back again. Maybe if my face hadn't been frozen into a ridiculous Jenny face while I was playing, it wouldn't have been such a dead giveaway. In any case, I think I've given up disguises for the time being.

HATING HEATHER LOCKLEAR

I've always tried to spread the word to young girls that perfection does not exist when it comes to the human body. Back when I was young, I used to hate Heather Locklear just because she looked so perfect. I was jealous. That's why I go overboard now to prove that I don't take myself too seriously. I think that by making fun of myself I'm showing girls that you don't always have to be perfect. Because—TRUST ME—no one is.

I mean, let's be honest here. I still have many things that I'm insecure about. I have stretch marks and cellulite, and I get cold sores once a month. But through the magic of airbrushing you see none of that. I wish I'd known that when I was young—I would have had so much more self-esteem if only I'd been aware that nobody was as perfect as they looked in the magazines.

So be proud of who you are, kids! You're worth it!

be proud of who you are

My *Three* Biggest
Beauty Tips

1

Don't wash your hair every day. Do it three times a week at most. No more, even if you're tempted and your head starts itching. Not washing your hair more than three times a week keeps those all-important oils in your hair without making you look like you're a total greaser.

2

Screw expensive soaps that come with fancy French names and designer prices. Trust me—Dove is what works for your face.

3

The most important trick to staying lean and mean is to have a good spiritual adviser, real or imagined, who can lead you to proper beauty and diet habits. Mine is Ronald McDonald.

trip

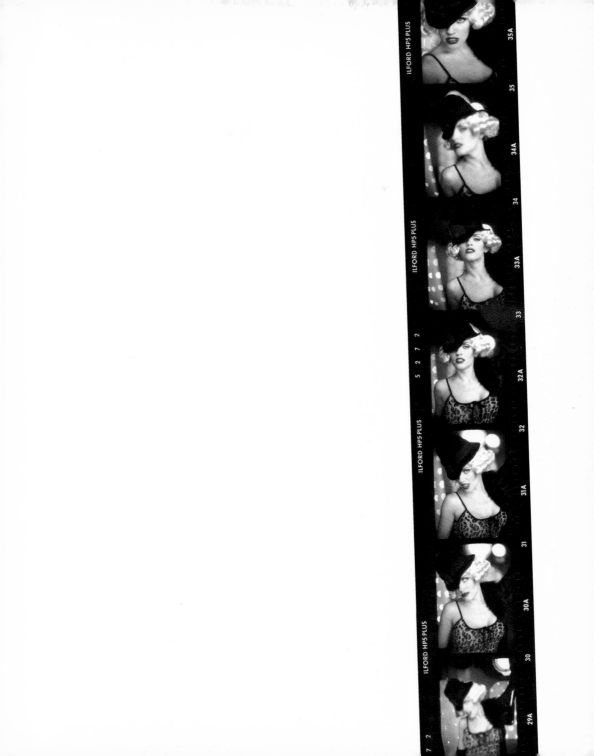

FROM B-LIST TO A-LIST

One of the strangest parts of being suddenly well known is that out of nowhere I now get invited to places where they would have called security on me only a few weeks before. Take last fall, when I got to go to dinner with President Bill Clinton and two hundred of his closest friends (okay, so it was actually a fund-raiser, and I had to pay $5,000 to go).

Still, this was a pretty small affair as presidential dinners go. The smallness meant, among other things, that everybody could meet the president and get their picture taken with him. Well, of course everybody in the waiting line was frothing with excitement—"Oh, my God, the president, oh, my God!" seemed to be the favored expression.

For once, and for reasons I don't understand, I wasn't totally goo-goo starry-eyed at meeting a real president. I mean, I met Bill Clinton, and he seemed like a really nice guy and all. He really has been blessed with a great presence. He seemed normal, and I felt kind of sorry for him because he looked so damned tired.

Like I said, having an unbelievable amount of attention thrust upon you all of a sudden can be bizarre. Only a year ago I was still going out on auditions for certain things where there would be two hundred girls who looked just like me waiting to audition for the same part.

Trying to stick out from the bunch is extremely hard in those circumstances. Suddenly, everyone thinks I'm special—or maybe crazy.

It's a weird feeling, especially after I'd spent decades having people think of me as a loser who deserved to be treated like dog poo. Even in my wildest fantasies I thought it would take me at least ten years to really make it the way I already have, in the manner I always wanted.

Someday, I'd always hoped, I would be perceived as fun, crazy, smart, outgoing, and one of the girls. Instead, that's happening now. I feel like people are beginning to understand the personality that's really inside me, not just the outline of my body. That's cool to me, very cool.

Not that I was ever running for the title of queen of cool. I'm more like the queen of the dorks, a royal ruler whose presence proves that it's okay to act like a nerd or make fun of yourself. Cool is definitely not something I'm trying to be . . . or ever really want to be.

MY FAVORITE COMEDY

I've always loved *Private Benjamin*, and not just because Goldie Hawn gave the performance of her life here as a bubbleheaded suburban princess who enlists in the army and is instantly humiliated in her initiation. (In fact, the torture Goldie goes through in boot camp reminds me a lot of my own high school experience.)

I think it's cool how Goldie shows a mixed-up girl who is somehow able to find direction and self-esteem in her life doing something no one thinks she can succeed at. Hmm. Sounds a little like me.

I also think it's cool that Goldie produced this movie herself. Someday I'm going to do that too.

THE WALK OF FAME

It still sounds really weird when people refer to me as "famous" or a "celebrity." Because I really don't feel like I'm a star. My ambitions have always been so high that I won't be able to look in the mirror and say to myself, "Baby, you're a star!" until one thing happens.

The day I get my own star on the Hollywood Walk of Fame is the day I can really think of myself as an actual star. Until then, like everybody else, I'm just paying my dues.

AUTOGRAPH MY _ _ _ !

Well, surprise, surprise, I have had some weird fans. No John Hinckleys so far, thank God, but I'm very careful to be very careful. Probably the strangest fellow I ran into during my *Playboy* years was a guy who came to one of my magazine autographing sessions. There were four hundred people in line, as well as a healthy contingent of media and cameras, and this man walked up to me, pulled down his pants, and asked me to autograph his butt.

All I remember thinking was that this guy has got some kind of balls to do this in front of so many people. I've tried to repress the memory, but I can still recall his hairy butt and . . . eccch!

It's funny, because now I have fans who are little kids and don't know that I ever posed nude in *Playboy*, as well as followers who know me only as the Playmate of the Year. It's kind of ironic, the differences in the way they both perceive and approach me on the street.

As I've said, little girls tend to come up to me and say, "I love when you beat up the boys. I've always wanted to beat up the boys, but I can't. So in a way you do it for me."

The men who've never accepted that I've left *Playboy*, meanwhile, usually begin by saying, "Dude, you're soooo raw! That picture of you in *Playboy* on page 64 where you're wearing that . . . ? And looking like a . . . with that big . . . Oh, yeah! I can't believe I'm actually meeting the *Playboy* Playmate of the Year!"

Probably the weirdest fan I've had of late is a gentleman who wrote me at MTV a few months ago. He looked to be about forty-five from the picture he sent me; I didn't judge him just because he wrote that he still lived with his parents.

But that picture was a beaut. In it, the guy's hair is slicked back and he's wearing glasses with thick Coke-bottle lenses, as well as a *Star Trek* shirt. Surrounding the guy was a roomful of *Star Trek* memorabilia.

On top of the picture, the guy wrote: "I love you, Jenny." On the back he wrote: "P.S. I still wear my glasses." I loved that. That picture and letter are still hanging up on my refrigerator at home, where they will remain forever.

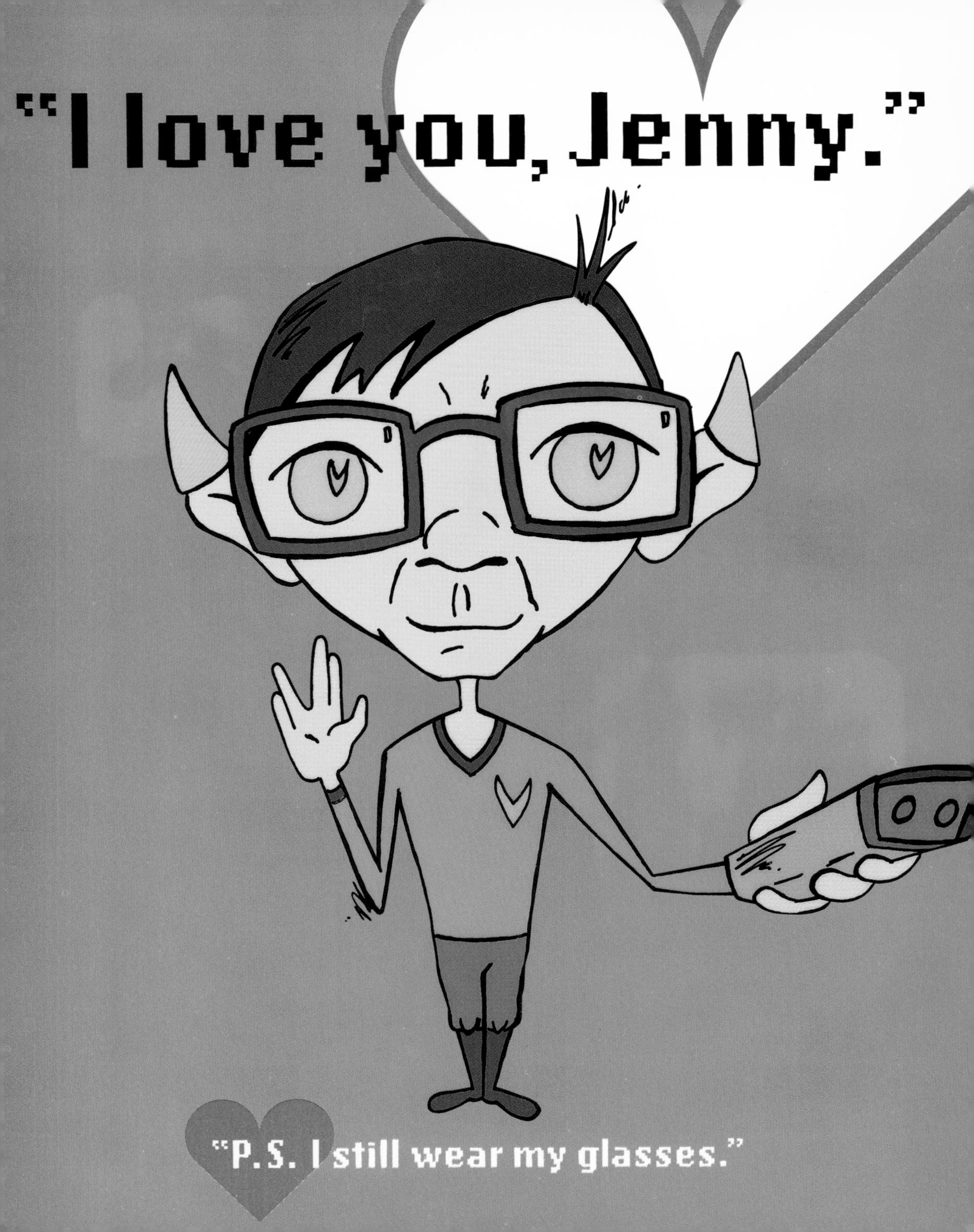
"I love you, Jenny."
"P.S. I still wear my glasses."

WHY I LOVE LUCY

Like I've said everywhere to everyone, Lucille Ball has always been my favorite comedian. Like me, she started out as a pinup girl with dyed hair who everybody thought was a brainless bimbo. Wrong, way wrong!

So, in preparation for writing this book, I thought it made sense to read Lucy's autobiography to see how my hero described the triumphs and tragedies of her life.

In there, she said something that so perfectly captured what I'm after as a comedian and actress that I thought I'd pass it along. "It is so important to have what I like to call the enchanted sense of play," Lucy said in 1959.

"Many, many times you should think and react as a child in doing comedy," she went on. "All the inhibitions and embarrassments disappear. We did some pretty crazy things in 'I Love Lucy,' but we believed every minute of them. It's like getting drunk without taking a drink."

Yes, Lucy!

A lot of times when I get home late from the set of my own sitcom I turn on Nick at Nite and study how Lucy did her comedy. Do you know a better comedy professor?

HOW I LIVE LUCY

Now, in describing my new sitcom on NBC, I tell everyone I want the feeling of the comedy on my show to be like Lucy's. Follow Jenny's madcap escapades as she tries to survive Hollywood with her best pal, Maggie!

Having my character working temp jobs around town is a nice setup for some very Jenny-like adventures. Whether I'm working in a copy shop like Kinko's or deciding to have my tongue pierced, I'm dealing with the grave issues of the day. Not.

But it's funny. It's an apt premise, having me play a transplant from Utica, New York, who's inherited her late father's house in Los Angeles. And George Hamilton is great as my dead dad, a B movie actor who speaks to his daughter through a series of video wills and old films he's left behind. The reason I'm really excited about this show is I'll get to to show the *other* side of Jenny—the emotional, sincere side.

MAKE A FACE

Not so long ago, I got kind of sick of always appearing in magazines with my mouth open and my face twisted into some goofy expression. I really don't think of myself as someone who "does" faces; in my mind that's something best left to Jim Carrey.

My co-star Heather Paige Kent and me

Still, you will see a lot of pictures of me in a beautiful gown, my hair all made up, topped off by me making a ridiculous face. It all started as a kind of joke to me, as my little comment on all those Hollywood people who like to pose for the photographers outside of restaurants or at awards ceremonies as if they were the most glamorous people since Marilyn Monroe or Clark Gable.

Well, for me, twisting my mouth around was my way of kind of making fun of that attitude—and making fun of myself. The problem was, however, that those faces soon became all that the paparazzi wanted from me every time I went through one of their little lines.

"Jenny, come on, do something goofy. We don't want you to just stand there!" the photographers would yell at me when I tried to confront their flashbulbs like a normal Hollywood person.

So I would say, "No, my mom wants a picture of me with just a smile, so just go ahead and take the picture this way."

And they never do. They won't take that normal picture. Instead, they'll just wait around for me to do my face number. Until now, I've almost always given in to them and ultimately thrown them whatever pose they wanted. Then they'd take that picture and run it over and over in their magazines, ad infinitum and ad nauseam. What can you do?

If you piss off the paparazzi, they'll just follow you around until they catch you in curlers and sweatpants with your finger up your nose. But then again, that would be okay with me too. So time and again, I'd surrender and make the face. That's the reason virtually every picture you might have seen of me during the last couple of years showcases me doing my rubber-mouth number.

Still, I think people have seen enough of those shots, so all that kind of stuff is going to end pretty soon. It's time to move on.

One of the worst parts of show business is dealing with the constant lies and false

rumors spread by people who are either bored, jealous, or just out to get you. This is where my training in the battleground of Mother McAuley parochial school was very helpful.

I mean, how much can a rumor that I'm sleeping with Chris Hardwick of *Singled Out* hurt when long ago the girls at my high school were spreading tales that I was sleeping with the entire football team?

So, by the time I got out here, I was already pretty used to how people can lie, and was able to deal with all that without freaking out.

There is also a common misconception that I'm this wild party animal, a real bad girl who loves to go out on the town and do the macarena on tabletops. In truth, I like to stay home when I'm not working. My favorite pastime is to do absolutely nothing but read books, play with my dog, and go to the movies.

I know that's kind of boring; my true habits don't make for hot copy. So every once in a while, just to stir things up, I do find that it helps to get away and do the macarena. Is that a crime, especially if no one gets hurt?